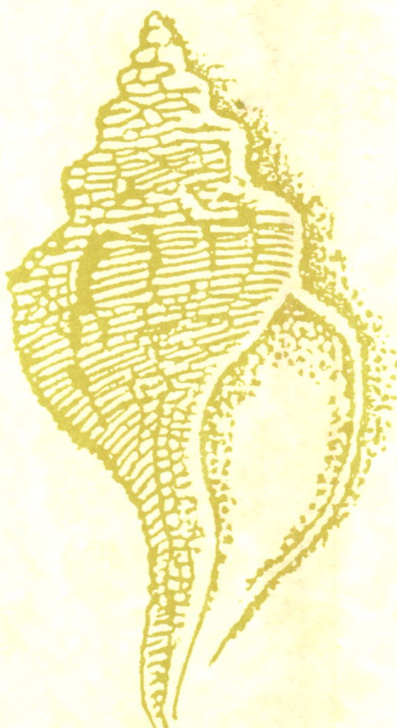

THE NATURE OF MAN AND CULTURE

THE NATURE OF MAN AND CULTURE

ALTERNATIVE PARADIGMS IN ANTHROPOLOGY

Edited by
BAIDYANATH SARASWATI

INDIRA GANDHI NATIONAL CENTRE FOR THE ARTS
NEW DELHI

ARYAN BOOKS INTERNATIONAL
NEW DELHI

The Nature of Man and Culture

ISBN-81-7305-196-8

Published in **2001** by
INDIRA GANDHI NATIONAL CENTRE FOR THE ARTS
Central Vista Mess, Janpath, New Delhi-110 001 (India)
and
ARYAN BOOKS INTERNATIONAL
Pooja Apartments, 4B, Ansari Road, Darya Ganj, New Delhi-110 002 (India)
Tel. : 3287589, 3255799, Fax : 91-11-3270385

Computer Typeset at ABI Prints & Publishing Co., New Delhi
Printed in India at B.B.N. Printers, New Delhi

CONTENTS

PART IV. QUESTION OF UNIVERSALITY

CONTRIBUTORS

BAIDYANATH SARASWATI
Unesco Professor, Indira Gandhi National Centre for the Arts, New Delhi

MAKHAN JHA
Professor, Ranchi University, Ranchi

N.K. BEHURA
Professor, Utkal University, Bhubaneshwar

A.R. MOMIN
Professor, Bombay University, Mumbai

ONKAR PRASAD
Professor, Visva Bharati University, Santiniketan

MOLLY KAUSHAL
Research Associate, Indira Gandhi National Centre for the Arts, New Delhi

OSAGA ODAK
Professor, University of Nairobe, Kenya

J. McKIM MALVILLE
Professor, University of Colorado, USA

S.C. MALIK
Professor, Nehru Memorial Museum, New Delhi

ANJALI CAPILA
Reader, Lady Irwin College, New Delhi

YOLOTL GONZÁLEZ TORRES
Director, Centre of Asian Studies, Ibero American University, Mexico City

RAFAEL LOPEZ-SANZ
Professor, Central University of Venezuela, Caracas

HAN SANG-BOK
Professor, Seoul National University, Korea

JAN BROUWER
Director, Centre for Advanced Research on IKS, Mysore

INTRODUCTION

• Anthropology As Question

The 14th International Congress of Anthropological and Ethnological Sciences was held in the city of Williamsburg, Virginia, on July 26 - August 1, 1998. Being the last of the 20th century, this conference was subtitled 'The 21st Century : The Future of Anthropology'. It was both witness and tribute to the late 20th century theory of anthropology, with the stress on new frontiers. The Indira Gandhi National Centre for the Arts organized a scientific session aimed at searching alternative paradigms in the study of man and culture. A body of knowledgeable experts explored challenges and prospects of integrating indigenous knowledge with anthropological perceptions of the west. The proceeding of this session comprise this volume.

Anthropology, based on the premises of a materialistic science, does not answer but raises questions about man. As for secular Western science, what is one to think? Are other modes of thinking possible outside this horizon? Are there no other visions of man, no other pillars of truth? Must everything be aided only by reason? Must everyone be converted to the Western way of thinking and living? Must an African, an Indian, a Chinese be uprooted from the nature-integrated culture created by an original act? Should one claim superiority over such people and culture as are subject to anthropological study? Can a researcher studying the Other be objective? Can a scientific observation disregard the observing mind? Can one observe the hidden variables of another culture? Do we have to follow the Darwinian-Tylorian-Durkheimian-Morganian-Malinowskian anthropology, with no real choice at all? Or do we look for a new understanding?

The quantum theory has taken physics far beyond Newton. Heisenberg's 'uncertainty principle' puts an end to the clear separation between the observer and the observed. Paradigms of physics, cosmology and biology are becoming a close companion of ancient philosophy and religion. Anthropology, the science of man, nurtured by evolutionism, materialism and colonialism, must give up the materialistic doctrine "to turn to the people". Materialism dominates anthropology. Cultures are classified by economic differences and the gap between the 'developing' and the 'developed' is widening. Traditional cultures have rejected scientific value of 'colonial anthropology'. For a new social order, a new anthropology has to make its appearance. The old assumptions will have to be abandoned. New paradigms must widen the dimension of universality. Only then can the core truth about the nature of man and culture find expression. Perhaps, the term 'quantum anthropology' will replace the shadowy anthropology marked by paradoxical conjustions of matter and spirit, myth and science, the observer and the observed, the developed and the developing. The materialistic secular Western perception is limited by human senses. Aware of this predicament we will have to widen the realm of all possibility.

- Sacred Science

Anthropology has distanced itself from natural philosophy. There are two incompatible maxims—*culture ex cultura* and *culture ex natura*. Culturalists grant cultural phenomena as autonomous and efficient agent of themselves. Naturalists, on the other hand, attribute cultural forms to Nature, i.e. cultural forms have evolved from Nature. In other words, culture is a step beyond Nature. Both these perceptions have given rise to what might be called the 'ladder mentality'. The ladder symbolizes a climb through simple to complex, from instinct to intelligence, from non-living to living, from less conscious to more conscious, from inorganic elements to plants to animals to humans; also from disorder to order. In each case this world is pinned to a ladder of progressive development. The polaristic position in the anthropological theory of Nature and Culture, is nullified by the 'sacred science of man'. Nature in its essence is not a machine. Living matter exists only by the order of the 'transcendent life', the one which is formless, invisible, but knowable through its effect. The transcendent Order of Nature is that (*prakriti*) which may appropriately be described as process; that Order of orders is set into a technical order that causes bio-social types. Traditional thought differentiates, but does not separate. Evolutionism, structuralism and functionalism are not applicable to non-Western 'sacred science'. The following articles by Indian anthropologists try to introduce, primarily by example, the non-Western concepts.

The contribution of Saraswati is an overview of the field of 'sacred science'. Here the entire oppositional category, used in Western-oriented anthropology, merges into a unity of thought. The emphasis is on the essence of relationship, felt and expressed by alternative interpretation of the order of things. The relation that expresses the 'ultimate constitution of reality' is one, the all-embracing. And hence: one as many, man as microcosm, science as society, theodicy as cosmodicy, mind as matter, word as world, knowledge as experience, knowledge as culture, nature as culture, ritual as language, tradition as hierohistory, etc. It is on these premises that indigenous cultures stand and the cosmic anthropological principle is born into. Traditional thought transcends modern fundamental dichotomies: man/nature, subject/object, individual/society, atomistic/holistic, relative/absolute, reality/symbol, sacred/secular, thinker/thought, creator/created, man/god and so on. This problem is posed as a challenge to the secular Western anthropology.

The paper by Jha provides a deeper appreciation of the sacred science of man. In order to grasp the nature of man one must go back to traditional thought which is reflective or philosophical. The author demonstrates that Indian philosophy, astrology, and *ayurvedic* system of medicine—whereby the experience of culture is codified—view man and his nature in a holistic perspective, irrespective of ethnic considerations. Human nature in its richness and variety, in its heights and depths, in its psychophysical expression, and in its spiritual transcendence along its vertical plane is at once attractive and baffling.

Behura's article takes the discussion on man further along the same line. Basing himself on transcendent ontology, the author explains how the Hindu concept of Self is manifest in people's punctuated lifestyle. The statement that humans in Indian society assert personal independence and freedom is an effective rallying point in the 'sacred science of man'. The ultimate reality perceived in Indian thought is at once cosmic, social and individual.

The article by Momin draws attention to philosophical anthropology. The fact that there is a sharp distinction between Islamic epistemology and Cartesian-Newtonian world-view exposes the limitations of modern science. The discourse of Sufism in Islamic 'sacred science' presents a new vision for the study of human nature and behavior. Western anthropology has paid little attention to the non-Western conception of human nature. Since the problem of human nature lies at the heart of anthropology, it is worthwhile to examine alternative views.

Prasad's paper presents a model for a new anthropology of sound. Highlighting the importance of the Upanisadic 'sacred science', the author assesses the Santhal theory of sound inhering the basic principle of differentiation as well as unification of all things. It shows that sound is causal to the cosmological process of creation, dissolution and re-creation. This perception of the so-called 'tribal' culture shows that the simple folk has an extraordinary capacity for integrating the complex phenomena of the natural world. The modern visualization of sound is different.

- Space And Time

Traditional cultures view space and time as reality, originating from the First cause and the First effect. For some cultures man moves through space and hence the primacy of spatial experience. For others, man moves through time and hence the importance of the present moment. At a higher level of mystic experience, it is said, man is not limited by space and time. All cultures hold that man's relationship with space and time is organic. Man is bound up in this world by physical space and temporal time. The finite space he occupies and the finite time he lives are the rhythms of the infinite cosmic spacetime balanced by a higher order (of divinity) perceived differently in different cultures. Hence traditional cultures refer to the spiritual potency of space (sacred space) and time (auspicious time) and the ultimate merging into Great Time (Mahakala) and the unfolding of the universe of space and time (by Narayan initiating the process of creation). Both sacred and secular sciences share an idea of interdependency of space and time. Significantly, modern man's attitude towards Nature—his passionate possession of space and time-measured personal identity—cannot reach the depth of aesthetic sensibility of the natural world. For instance, bathing in a sacred river at an auspicious time is an extraordinary experience utterly strange to the modern secular man.

Kaushal's contribution is notable for its manner of interpreting the traditional vision of space and time. Apart from its wealth of information about the Gaddis of India, the paper presents a symbolic system which creates categories of space and time in terms of a (masculine-feminine) continuum. Within this framework of thought, space and time are inherently pure, non-contaminated and auspicious. Both, as power of God (Shiva-Parvati), constitute the absolute principle by which the Gaddi culture interprets its existence. The idea of interrelationship between space and time, developed along the metaphor of seed and womb (which makes the living world) and stitched together in the warp and woof of creation and dissolution (which makes the natural world) sacred and secular (which makes the socialworld), maintains the idea of justice or balance. This thought pattern is explained geometrically (sacred geometry) and numerically (sacred number).

Odak's article starts with the premise that there is a relationship between space, time and technology. It shows that modern technology remains a challenge which traditional societies have not yet been able to meet. The distructive nature of culture determines the concept of space. For instance, the difference between the First World and Third World cultures is marked in terms of their conception of space and time. This is precisely because they are placed at two different levels of technological advancement. African culture conceives of space in circular or oval shape and measures time in approximation based on the observation of the heavenly bodies. African society today is subjected to conflicting forces, but African space and time integrate the people. The technocentric modern space and time, on the contrary, tend to isolate the individual.

Yet another contribution to the volume was by a leading astrophysicist Malville who presents a new vision for anthropology of pilgrimage (sacred spaces). His investigation reveals that traditional village cultures and the world-spanning pilgrimage are self-organized, self-similar systems. The complexity of the pilgrimage landscape may be transformed by a robustly open system that is holistic, complex in space and time, and quick to change. Biological and spiritual impulses that disrupt equilibrium derive cultural systems into new realms by causing metastability. Some systems such as the traditional village may maintain stability through an enhancement of feedback loop when threatened by destablizing forces.

- EXPERIENCE AND EXPRESSION

An experimental scientist such as a chemist uses the method of laboratory experiment. For an anthropologist fieldwork is a substitute for the experimental laboratory. But, like a chemist, can he claim objectivity in his research? Is he not an aspect of the human reality which he studies? Is intellect only a knowing mind? Can one say that empirical data are bare facts? Is mere observation of the object enough to know? The answer to all these questions is in negative. The human mind cannot remain impersonal, objective; it blends the object with subjectivity. An anthropologist has to be necessarily involved at personal level to judge or sense the empirical reality, and thus he gains experience and knowledge. No participant observation can be done by proxy. No culture can be comprehended mechanically. The inescapable conclusion is that anthropological study leads to both, knowing and experiencing the reality. As it shows, experience cannot be expressed totally. An authentic experience is ineffable. There is a dichotomy between experience (sensory consciousness) and expression (reflection of experience).

The expression has to be differentiated from its interpretation (intellectual consciousness). Briefly the state of experience does not remain the same at the level of expression and explanation. However, each culture interprets its own 'lived experience' in the light of its particular cultural codes. A study of symbolic structures of cultural experience is necessary to move from a formal analysis of material culture to the 'lived experience' of a culture.

Malik's model for 'anthropology of experience', marked by the subtlety of expression, bears out the validity of his approach. It proceeds from the premise that 'the knowledge we formulate about the other is filtered or refracted through the knowledge we have built for ourselves, i.e. we are interpreters of cultures and can observe others only through our own cultural and experiential biases'. To provide a warning to anyone embarking on this approach, it emphasizes that 'the human approach to a cultural model must encompass all experience. One can of course only attempt to approximate the verbal and non-verbal experiences in terms of the shared experience, and as far as possible it is to share emotions—if at all in any case . May be there can be lived understanding of the situation, event and process.'

Capila addresses to the same concern : participant observation as 'lived experience'. Based on her fieldwork in Garhwal Himalaya, the author demonstrates that among the traditional women singers the 'lived experience' is not restricted to the personal self, as in modern societies. Songs are to be understood as a matter of actual experience, also of participation.

The paper of Gonzalez Torres deals with the spiritual experience—communicating with the cosmos by worshipping the supernatural. Her study of Mexican dance and ritual shows that even today the dancers express their emotions and develop a sense of identification with the ancient Mexican culture.

• Question Of Universality

Human cultures originate from various places on earth and develop in many ways. Culture types are more varied than human biological types. However, their differences can be modified, expanded and transformed. These cultures are changing constantly. If behaviour patterns and language make up a culture, then again, there are many, many forms of culture. Thus one can draw that culture is the source of division and change. Like flowering plants in nature, the formation and transformation of a culture takes place in an almost mystical way. Should a culture seek to have relevance in modern time, it has to address itself to a radical cross-cultural problem. Only those cultures which are intelligible to Western civilization and its colonies will find a place in the horizon of universality. Others will have to renounce their claim to possess the universal nature of culture. The early evolutionists placed many primitive societies under pre-cultural stage. In the world-view of Judeo-Christian civilization, which is associated with the colonialist pattern of expansion, the indegenous peoples are pre-civilized. In the situation, can anthropology develop a universal language?

In his paper Lopez-Sanz, situating his discourse in the post-modern scenario, brings out the contributions and problems and failings of anthropology since its inception. At the present moment, animated by the modernity/postmodernity working paradox, he envisages the role of the Third World as one of interlocutor-translator mediating between its inhabitants and passions, fighting cultural boundaries and situations of crisis.

Sang-Bok's paper presents a critical review of the development of Euro-American anthropological theories that fulfilled the need of colonial rulers and reflected the American social, economic and political situations. He examines the work of Chinese anthropologist Fei Xiatong's 'peoples anthropology', which aimed at making the masses understand the society they live in, to organize their collective life in accordance with existing social laws and to help satisfy their ever-growing needs. The emphasis of 'people's anthropology' is on ethical issues.

Brouwer's essay starts with a historical review of the crisis of interpretation and proceeds further to formulate an alternative paradigm in anthropology. He recommends the collection and authentication of indigenous knowledge in its cognitive and practical dimensions at the confluence of concepts originating in different knowledge systems with people's active participation in collection and preservation'.

• Towards A New Relationship

What comes out of this meditation upon the many aspects of anthropology from the perspective of many nations and scholars can become a starting point for establishing a new relationship with the intellectual heritage of the past. This is possible only through participation in the mystery of cosmodicy. As it appears from the essays collected here, the traditional vision of man is still being re-stated and re-interpreted with clarity and vision in many parts of the world where the objectivist anthropology, which is neither clear nor constant, is challenged openly. This search for alternative paradigms in anthropology indicates that the non-Western anthropologists are fully aware that it is time to write the fate of their culture directly from a source that existed in the pre-Renaissance Europe. Before asking what conclusions are to be drawn, it is important to understand that the traditional vision contains potentials which become actualized as comprehensive thought which then becomes cohesive concept. An effort to 're-language' traditional thought in terms of 'sacred science', 'cosmic anthropology', 'sonic anthropology', 'philosophical anthropology', 'quantum anthropology', 'experiential anthropology', 'people's anthropology', and so on will eventually make it possible to conceive anew the true nature of man and culture.

Spring 2000. **Baidyanath Saraswati**

PART I

SACRED SCIENCE

1

ALTERNATIVE PARADIGMS IN ANTHROPOLOGY: THE COSMIC ANTHROPOLOGICAL PRINCIPLE

Baidyanath Saraswati

• Background

The history of anthropology is associated with colonial expansion. With the end of colonial rule emerged new thoughts in the minds of those whose cultures had been subjected to a disgraceful generalization. As they awoke, they found that anthropology had caused a misunderstanding of the universal nature of culture, that its empirical scientism was banal and that it projected a world-view in which Nature was a hostile force which must be kept at bay.

Is anthropology a 'chosen' science of man? Do anthropologists have a special gift, a particular grace, that has not been given to others? Is anthropology a discipline of infinite curiosity only about non-Western cultures? Can anthropology lay claim to universality? Is the notion of universality universal? These questions can be answered by saying that the search for new paradigms is a cultural imperative. A paradigm is not a theory but a framework for thought, a conceptual scheme around which empirical data are organized.

India came under the strong-arm of British rule in 1857. A clever attempt was made to gather full account of the people of India. Descriptive ethnology, classified under 'tribe' and 'caste', was pinned to a 'ladder of progressive development'. That marked the beginning of anthropology in India. There is nothing in Indian thought or in the social organization of its tradition that may correspond to the evolutionary notion of the primitive 'tribe'. The 'tribe' exists in India as an administrative category created by the British Raj, intellectualized by anthropologists and sanctified by the Constitution of modern India.

During colonial rule, Darwinian anthropology became the paradigm or lens, through which all perspectives about Indian society and culture were formed. The major emphasis was on descriptive accounts of 'quaint' customs and beliefs, 'purity' and 'pollution'. Traditional thought was branded as a collection of empty concepts. An utter disrespect for India's traditional knowledge resonates in Macaulay's remark, 'All the books written in the Sanskrit language are less valuable than what may be found in the most paltry abridgement used at preparatory schools in England'.

In the field of theory, the position of Indian anthropology has been colonial in relation to the schools which have dominated the European and American scenes from time to time. Indian scholars were chiefly collectors of descriptive data. As a consequence, no endogenous insights could develop. There are only a few exceptions, such as S.C. Roy, N.K. Bose and G.S. Ghurye, who tried to seek new directions in cultural anthropology. Indologists such as V. Raghavan and others have influenced a community of anthropologists identified with what might be called the Chicago School of Indian Anthropology. Among Western scholars who have attempted a realistic delineation with an authentic concrete sense of India, McKim Marriot has made a name for himself. His recent work on 'Constructing an Indian Ethnosociology' shows his full comprehension of the inner meaning of Indian thought.

This sketchy description of the overall trend is obviously a retrograde step. When I think back to what had gone on in the field of anthropology, I realize that many of our problems today have their roots in the decennial censuses carried out by anthropologists. The partition of the country, the linguistic conflict, the 'tribal' unrest, the separatist religious movements, the caste cynicism, followed by corrupt politics and unstable governments, measure the trace of the anthropology of British India.

Now it turns out that the real problem is methodological rather than a geographical antithesis. Indian anthropologists have been studying their own cultures, many of them have made use of Sanskrit and other traditional sources, and yet the chaos in Indian anthropology is compounding. My contention is that it will make no difference whatsoever unless traditional cosmology and ontology serve as the framework of anthropological thought. This means a return to the old truth.

From the turn of the 1970s, I have been pleading trans-anthropologization, which means deconstruction of the colonial anthropology and re-anthropologization, i.e., construction of a new anthropology. More cheering appears to my work at the Indira Gandhi National Centre for the Arts, inspired by Kapila Vatsyayan, which has initiated a deep and meaningful discourse on the fundamental concepts of Space, Time, Nature, Culture, Man, Mind, Order; and all that. What I am considering in this presentation is a specific paradigm *inherent* in Indian thought. This will hopefully lead us to a progressive realization of the presence of the One in all cultures, throughout the universe.

• The Sacred Science Of Man

Indian tradition speaks of thought (or thinking about thought) as a transcendent phenomenon in the scheme of things. One of the earliest works on human organization is the *Manav Dharma Shastra*, literally the 'Sacred Science of Man'. This text is the Word of *Manu*, the First Man. It symbolizes the principle or Law of Life. *Manu* is the symbol of the universal consciousness which exists in the transcendent, and also in the differentiated units of creation, or in each individual centre which is but a ray from its source, the universal Sun. *Manu* is the Mind of the Creator, the principle of Ego. The Mind of the Creator is an ocean, of which the measure of Death is too profound to be known or comprehended by anyone. What he planned in his Mind, he executed in his creation. There is a complete identity between the Creator and the cosmos. *Manu* has a twofold aspect. He is above Time and Space and he is also the presiding ruler of each cosmic cluster of Time. Each *Manu* is the sovereign ruler of his dynastic Time and it is his charge that the primeval ordinance be fully and perfectly fulfilled in his period. It is the *Manu*-Principle that governs Indian vision and society.

There is another principle which touches on a crucial problem that could easily be the starting point for understanding Man and his Universe. It is the Matter Principle of fundamental Elements in their gross and subtle aspects of the reality. The third is the Creating Principle, which is the cause and the ultimate basis of the world. These three interrelated principles are set in motion from the beginning of the world to descend into the sacred history of Man and thereby into the present time. What we seek to indicate is that the Sacred Science proceeds from another source of knowledge, which is infinite, and that it is continually transmitted to this world to the extent to which Man has not ceased to read the signs.

Here we deal with a set of pairs of conceptual categories of Sacred Science discourses, which merge into a unity of thought, quite different from the anthropological conception of binary opposites.

• One As Many

The Upanishadic sages had described *brahman* as *bindu*, the dimensionless point, literally a drop. The *bindu* consists of the unity of two: one static and the other dynamic. It is the dynamic aspect that expresses itself as the Universe of multiplicity, but it essentially remains One, the epitome of all. In geometry the point is the Sun, i.e., the centre with a circumference. There is a centre and a periphery, diameter and radius. The circle is a point expanded: the meeting of four equal lines forms a square, and three lines come together to form a triangle. These primary forms are fundamental to Hindu thought.

The concept of *shunya*, zero, when applied to *brahman*, the Absolute, is unthinkable in itself. Metaphysically it is identified with both fullness and emptiness. The description of *brahman* as full and empty shows that it is beyond the dialectical oppositions of time and timelessness, formed and unformed, mortal and immortal, actual and beyond; and so on. The whole Universe is regarded as a living organism. The *Hiranyagarbha*, the Golden Egg, is a cosmic metaphor attributed to the origin of the Universe. Here gold symbolizes the principle of light shining forth from within the womb of darkness. The sap within the Egg originally existed in an undifferentiated form but later were born the seven primeval Ancestors, or seven differentiated life forces (Mind, Life, and the Five Elements of Matter). The Egg floated in Waters for a thousand years and then something triggered off. It split into two and the whole Universe came into existence.

The organic units of the Universe are further clarified by an anthropic metaphor. From the limbs of *Purusha*, the Cosmic Man, everything originated: strophes and melodies, horses and every animal, the four human castes, the Sky, the atmosphere, the Ocean, the Earth, the Moon, the Sun, the Fire, the Wind and the King of Gods. The idea of organic relationship is pursued to a high degree of sophistication. It recurs in the *Brihadaranyaka Upanishad*:

> The Self is the honey of all beings
> and all beings are honey for the Self.

The mathematical description of *brahman* as zero reveals what is infinite.

a-a=o; a+o=a; a-o=a; a x o=o; a ¸ o becomes infinity.

The geometric description highlights the plurality of primary forms: the square, the circle and the triangle. In the description of the Cosmic Egg or Man, the One is not the all, that is, the One is not the sum total; the One subsists in the many. Although the world of plurality has emerged out of the One, the One is not affected by the defects of the many. Here, the

One is to be understood as a dimension of the Self. The primordial oneness arises from within the Self, hence it makes differentiation possible. The individual Self is valuable precisely because all generic and ontic differences are included in the One, the universal Self.

• Man As Microcosm

Anthropologists' conception of Man is grounded in the theory of evolution. In biology, evolution refers to slow changes in the process of growth. Applied to human evolution, it implies that Man represents the pinnacle of evolution and his world is pinned to a ladder of progressive development.

Today, evolutionists and creationists are in the midst of a continuing ideological struggle. The supporters of 'scientific creationism', which developed in America in the early 1970s, say the following: 'Evolution and creation are competing scientific models. Since evolution is merely a model, and is not testable by experimentation, one must have faith that it is true. If an alternative model for Nature would correlate the facts better than the evolution model, then it would be the one to believe'.

There is another theory which looks inward upon Man and the Universe. Its basic assumption is that, like the rest of the material world, Man's body is made up of the Five Primordial Elements: (i) Earth, (ii) Water, (iii) Fire, (iv) Air and (v) Sky. Each major organ is said to have its own builder. Head and ears are associated with Sky, neck and chest with Air, stomach with Fire and body with Earth. The five fingers, from the little finger to the thumb, are associated with Earth, Water, Fire, Air and Sky, respectively. Elements are also known to have caused the origin of bio-social types. For example, ironsmiths relate themselves with Earth, carpenters with Water, coppersmiths with Fire, sculptors with Air, and goldsmiths with Sky.

The theory of the Five Elements leaps forward to the vision of the Five 'sheaths' or envelopes: (i) the gross body or the vegetative envelope; (ii) the vital body; (iii) the mental body; (iv) the poetic or higher intellectual envelope and (v) the beatific envelope, which is the highest in the realization of self-knowledge and self-control.

Man's relationship with the Universe is explained by a powerful imagery of the cosmic Man, with a thousand heads, a thousand eyes and a thousand feet, encompassing the planet Earth on all sides and exceeding it by ten fingers' breath. This does not make the world anthropocentric. The Cosmic Man is neither being nor non-being. From him the shining cosmic Egg was born, and from this again he himself emerged. In other words, he became the creature of his own creation. From this creature the four human castes or classes (*varnas*) took birth. All creatures emanating from the cosmic body are invested with cosmic powers and functions.

Clearly, this perception of Man as microcosm is different from what the theories of evolution and creation claim.

• Science As Society

The *Manu*-Principle connects biology with cosmology. All life operates at the level of existence. Life and Death together form a continuum. All contingent beings originate from Space and to Space they return. Movement is a feature common to all beings. What moves is the individual Self, not the body. What dissolves is the body, not the Self. With this principle came the notion of human deeds and reincarnation.

The process by which man-woman, husband-wife originated relates to a cosmological principle. The One was the size of a man and a woman in close embrace. It split (*pat*) into two, and from that arose husband (*pati*) and wife (*patni*). Hence it is said: oneself is like half a potsherd. Husband and wife are indissolubly united. This has been expressed in several ways. Whatever the qualities of the man with whom a woman is united according to the Law, such qualities even she assumes, like a river united with the ocean.

He only is a perfect man who consists of three persons united: his wife, himself and his offspring. The theory of heredity is proclaimed. The woman is the soil, the man is the seed. The production of all corporeal beings takes place through the union of the soil with the seed. In some cases the seed is more distinguished and in some the womb of the female; but when the two are equal the offspring is most highly esteemed. On comparing the seed and the receptacle of the seed, the seed is declared to be more important; for the offspring of all created beings is marked by the characteristics of the seed.

The parent-child unity has been conceptualized in its genetic and spiritual oneness. As has been said: 'You move into the womb of *Prajapati* (the Father of all creatures). You yourself are born again'. The continuity of the Self conveys still another, though related, message. A child has two births even before he is actually born: the first in the state of the seed in the father and the second in which it enters the womb of the mother. The beauty of the relationship of the Self can be appreciated in this organized reasoning: 'He (the son) who is one self of his (father) is made his substitute (in the world) for (the performance of) meritorious deeds. Then the other self of his (father's) having done his duties, enters old age and departs. He as soon as departs from here, is born again. This is his (son's) third birth'.

The parent and the child form a continuity of the Self; and the husband, the wife and the offspring, a perfect unit. The unity is maintained in the lifetime and beyond Time (that is, even after Death) by performing the ancestral rite. 'The parent, being nourisher, should be nourished' is the ordinance. Kinship does not remain a mere societal relation between two living persons; it is the human energy conserved through generations. Kinship in this life may be much more complicated, but its continuity in the other world does not conflict with the fundamental Laws of energy. The Law of conservation of energy is as true for Life as for Matter.

The cosmic Principle of the One makes a complete sense in the fourfoldness of human organization. The imagery of the fourfold *varna* as the limbs (mouth, arms, legs, feet) of the Cosmic Man involves essentially an organic relationship. Each *varna* is a member of the personal aspect of the whole of reality. A *varna* is more than the sum total of all individuals: it subsists in many.

Human beings are classified into four categories, each *varna* being ordained to pursue a specific, hereditary, non-competitive occupation so as to ensure the harmony and prosperity of the Universe. This is comprehended along a line of continuum.

Human life is ordered into four stages. The life of a Brahman or a Kshatriya starts with learning and spiritual disciplining, rises to the culmination of worldly prosperity, retreats to the forest from where they had begun their intellectual journey, and finally forsakes all possessions and worldly emotional entanglement. The wholeness of life is maintained by performing evenly balanced roles at different stages. This scheme tallies with the Cosmic Law of return to the primordial. In the operational context of human organization, the system eliminates all possibility of generation gap.

Human desires are also classified into four categories: (i) the desire for righteousness in the sense of duty, (ii) the desire connected with wealth, (iii) the desire for pleasure and procreation and (iv) the desire for transcending all desires. The fulfilment of the fourfold desire is the approved goal of Life. Although contradictory in character, these desires stand in an organic and interactive relationship to one another; in effect they are counterpoised. The desire for 'wealth' and pleasure must be fulfilled, but strictly in accordance with the sense of duty. And the desire for the fulfilment of worldly duty must give way to liberation. This arrangement helps every individual feel satisfied and contented with the freedom and fullness of Life. It completes the cosmic rhythm and forms a single continuum of inward and outward.

- THEODICY AS COSMODICY

Christian theology considers Man as a special creation set apart from the rest of the animal kingdom which has been created to serve his needs and pleasure. Animals have no share in salvation, no position in eternity. Supporting the Christian theological explanation, Descartes reasoned that there was a qualitative and unbridgeable barrier between Man and Animal. Darwin took an antithetical view, as he brought up the subject of the origin and evolution of Life on Earth. He claimed to have proved his theory that no essential difference separated Man from other animals. The modern post-Christian West has overcome the two extremes by saying that Man is an animal but a very peculiar one, in many ways a unique animal. His uniqueness lies in his capacity for conceptual thinking, his cumulative tradition, his tools and his speech. Of his biological peculiarities, he is by far the most variable wild species, a dominant type and unique in the method of his evolution.

Cultures differ in their self-evaluation and understanding of the Other. Most cultures have traditionally maintained that a powerful bond exists between God (Spirit), Man and Animal. No one occupies a special place in the scheme of the Universe. No one is unique. All creatures have a completely cosmic origin in the self-designed Universe. One exists in relation to the other. All are subject to the eternal cycle of birth and death. The cosmic Law has no beginning, no end. It is boundless, but what comes out from the boundless is bounded. Thus it turns out that, technically speaking, all are 'reincarnated beings'.

The Hindus are antithetical of the theory of creation, and even more so of evolution, but are not opposed to the spirit of science in its original sense (*sapientia*). The picture of the Universe is painted as an expanding *brahman* with a centre. The first Three (God, Animal, Man) form a divine triangle on the surface of the Universe. They are the chief actors of this great theatre. Ocean cosmology links all of them in a remarkable way. The Cosmic Egg that lay within the 'womb' was the light of *brahman*, which is visible to us as Life. The auto-fission of the One (Cosmic Egg) caused the many. God Vishnu took incarnations. Of his ten complete incarnations, the first three were animal forms, the fourth was a composite form (animal-man), the fifth was a dwarf and the next four were fully developed humans.

Animals are not only the earliest form, they are also the most variable species living in varied ecological conditions of Water, Earth and Sky. Practically all conceivable forms of animals are associated with the Hindu pantheon —some as incarnations of God, others as God's vehicles. Each form is divine and unique in its genetic character and behavioural qualities. As God has assumed the powers of *brahman*, so have animals derived God's qualities and powers. Animals seem to have set standards for Man: in productive power; in swiftness, energy and strength; in mien and courage; in docility and inoffensiveness; in self-sacrificing quality; in artistic manifestation and beauty; in intelligence and faith; and so on. Ontological change in the moral order of time follows the degrees of respect for animals. Man is also a virtual animal (*pashu*, the 'roped' one). So are the Gods, because they are also 'roped' by the cycle of life and death. Hindu astrology makes Man intrinsically inseparable from an Animal. Every human being has two births, one from a human mother and another from a female animal, depending on the asterism at birth.

God, Animal and Man are not seen in terms of phylogeny. There is no path of evolution, no selection, no survival of the fittest. No species develop out of other species. The number of species is fixed. Each species is unique in itself. Eschatology provides the idea of inter-species biological connection outside Time, in no Time. It is the Soul, the Life-force, that switches from one form to another. Animal 'ancestors' (totems) play a decisive role in social life and ritual. Both God and Man may enter into animal species in their next births. The fortune of Men and of Gods is believed to be in the Animal. God and Man live in positive symbiosis with the animal world. Their purpose of existence is to maintain the original symmetry of the two worlds to which God provides supersymmetry.

• Mind As Matter

For Modern Science, Mind is a mere biological organism and has a purely physical basis. The Sacred Science offers a richer and more encompassing view of reality: 'In the beginning there was only Mind. That Mind created the Word. That Word created the Life-Breath. Beings are born from Mind, when born they live by Mind, on decease they enter into Mind. The body consists of Mind. Within the body, there is a lotus-shaped piece of flesh called the heart. The space within the heart is the permanent seat of the Mind. Mind is the agent in all conscious experience. Mind is the formless Matter. He who dwells in the Mind, is yet other than Mind, whom the Mind does not know, whose body is the Mind, who controls the Mind from within — He is the Self within you, the Inner Controller, the Immortal'.

It is at this level of thought that Mind is inseparable from Matter, Matter inseparable from Life, and Life inseparable from the universal Self.

Mind is of two kinds: pure and impure. It becomes impure when it is touched by desire and pure when it is freed from desire. When a Man, having made his mind perfectly stable, free from attachment and confusion, enters upon the 'mindless state', then he attains the supreme abode. The Mind alone is Man's cause of bondage or release; it leads to bondage when attached to the sense objects and to release when freed from them. As Saint Kabir has said:

> He who walks between boundaries is Man,
> he who goes beyond them is a saint.
> But he who transcends the limited and the limitless,
> his Mind is unfathomable.
>
> The body is a pitch dark forest and
> Mind is an elephant gone mad.
> The Jewel of Wisdom is the goad,
> but few are the saints who can apply it.
>
> The Three worlds were plundered,
> they all were stripped of their all.
> But Mind is a faceless Thief,
> whom no one could recognize.

Psychology is concerned with chaos in inner and outer realms. Chaotic behaviour contrasts with the ordered aspects of Life or Mind. But what may appear as chaotic outside is not necessarily continuous with the inside. There is another dimension to be considered and that is the spiritual Mind. An ascetic, at the mystical state of his consciousness, remains naked, eats like a cow, or lies down on his belly for eating, considers his body a corpse, and makes no social distinction of any kind. He is elevated to a higher state of pure consciousness. The outer chaos, or the absurdity of human existence, does not meddle with the blooming of his spiritual consciousness. At another level, Mind is both Cosmos and Chaos.

• Word As World

Tradition tells us in innumerable ways that Word is World. The Word, imperishable, is the First born of Truth. The Word is infinite and immense. All the Gods, the celestial Spirits, Men and Animals, live in the Word. In the Word all the worlds find their support. The Veda is not the Word of God. Nor it is inspired or authored by God. It is simply the primordial Word of which no human being is the author. This Word is the consort of the creator of the World. She was at the beginning. She is the source of human knowledge. She is the primordial mystery combining in herself the three worlds of Time: past, present and future. No wonder then, every Word is sacred and powerful.

The ultimate Reality is of the nature of 'Word-principle', and from it are manifested all the objects of the World, the whole Cosmos. The Word has been measured out in four degrees, three kept closely hidden; Men speak only the fourth degree of wisdom.

There are three aspects of the Word, three stages through which it passes whenever one speaks; that is, when the Word, which is at first quite internal, is externalized for the purpose of communication: (a) *Vaikhari*, the intoned Word, the most external stage when it is uttered by the speaker and heard by the hearer; (b) *Madhyama*, the middle one, going inward, the stage associated chiefly with the Mind, the intellect, and not with the organs of articulation; (c) *Pashyanti*, the seeing one, the innermost stage, which is said to have infinite varieties. It is also described as being of a lower and a higher kind. The higher kind is beyond the range of verbal usage; it is the highest dimension of the Word. Potentially, (a) could leap into (b), and (b) to (c). More correctly, there is a logical continuity between the levels of (a) and (b). At the level of (c) discontinuity begins. Also, (c) is doubly discontinuous with reference to (a) and (b), and with reference to the highest dimension of the Word. In the (b) stage there is no actual split or succession in the Word. The stage (c) is aware of itself. *Para*, the higher stage, is beyond such self-awareness. Or the self-awareness of the higher stage is (c).

Word as expressible experience originates in the twilight language of the non-manifest. To communicate their experience of 'seeing' the Word, the saints have developed a language of 'light-and-darkness' (*sandhyabhasa*) — partly light, partly darkness. It is also called the language of the 'inverted flute', the enigmatic, 'turned around' language. The sound of the 'inverted flute' is silence that measures the trace of what is in itself immeasurable. Kabir describes the power of the 'spoken' Word: 'In the one Word are thirty-six melodies; it makes the music infinite. God is the Letterless One'.

• Knowledge As Experience

As part of the modern systems of knowledge, anthropology prides itself in being *autotelic*, that is, human thought ought to be pursued for its own sake. This claim is consistent with the general theory of human evolution that makes Man the *telos* of his own thoughts, works and deeds. Man makes himself and his own history and civilization by virtue of his rational powers. He alone is the possessor of knowledge and the conqueror of Nature.

In the Indian theory of knowledge the key concept is 'cosmic Intelligence', which sustains the Life-force and vigour of all that exists. This divinity cannot be 'known', if by knowledge we understand a merely mental consciousness. It can be approached only by sacrifice, by holy action and by other means of entering into the 'womb' of the Ultimate. In other words, the primal knowledge is self-existent. At the human level it designates the cosmic process of knowing and also the result of it (acquired knowledge).

The other dimensions are: critical knowledge up to analytical consciousness, right knowledge, knowledge of the ultimate Reality (the total realization), knowledge of 'objective' Reality or true knowledge, and wisdom, or full consciousness. These categories stress a certain type of global knowledge. There is another set of concepts that emphasizes the type of more detailed and rational knowledge, vision, and perception. The third set relates to thinking, the process of knowing. The fourth group represents the world-view, the systematic vision of Reality, intellectual perception, dreams, mirror and doctrinal systems.

A mystical process of knowing the unknowable is reported from all traditional cultures. The process of experiencing is not just knowing; it means becoming part of the experienced object. By experience we understand immediate contact with the real. In the perfect experience there would be no difference between the experiencing subject and the experiencing object. Experience is untransferable and personal. It is said that the knower of the Ultimate becomes speechless. What this implies is this: Coming into direct contact with the source of knowledge, Man is elevated to a state of primordial consciousness where the knowable merges with the unknowable. There is much to do in this field of the anthropology of experience.

• Knowledge As Culture

Culture may be conceived of as a deposit of knowledge accumulated in space and time. The deposit of each culture is made up of two parts: 'manifest' and 'unmanifest'. The manifest part contains the knowledge of things revealed and discovered. The unmanifest part contains the beliefs and hopes of what is yet to be revealed and discovered. Revelation and discovery keep the manifest part in a state of flux; the unmanifest part remains in a perpetual state of mystification. Thus any classification of culture based on mere empirical content (that is, the manifest part) is bound to be partial and tentative. A relatively enduring and valid classification can be sought in terms of the modes of transmission of knowledge. There are three modes of transmission: (i) oral (*laukik*), (ii) textual (*shastriya*), and (iii) transcendental (*naivrittika*), each forming an organic unity of thought and action. Accordingly, there are Oral, Textual, and Transcendental cultures.

Based on personal factors in the development of thought, cultures are fourfold: (i) *Cosmocentric culture*, which recognizes the vital significance of cosmic Elements in the making of biological and cultural Man. (ii) *Theocentric culture*, which considers dissociation from the phenomenal world in favour of the divine eternal world as human perfection. (iii) *Anthropocentric culture*, which makes Man the measure of all and teaches a path to progress which is external to Nature. (iv) *Technocentric culture*, which worships technology in the belief and hope that higher possibilities of Man lie in affluence (temporal power), which is largely and necessarily a function of advancing technology. Of these, the first two types maintain that Life and culture originate dependently in the total context of divine Nature, which is changing and yet not changing. The path of human perfection lies within it: Man in harmony with Nature. In the other two types, there is a constructed environment unconnected with Nature, where the systems of Man and that of the machine are in conflict.

• Nature As Culture

The Newtonian view of Nature as a vast machine and the Darwinian conception of Nature as an evolutionary process remain deeply ingrained in Western thought and culture. Both involve some form of antithesis between the purely physical and the animate. In the former, it is a stark dichotomy between Matter and Mind; in the latter, it is the persistent contrast of organism to environment. The outcome is a 'culture of power and wealth', embodying the forces of colonization and 'ladder mentality'. Although the new physics and the new biology in our times have gone far beyond the old notions of materialism and evolutionism, there appears no concomitant change in the scientist's basic attitude towards Nature and culture.

There is another perception: Man *in* Nature. He sees Nature as his own self in becoming. He is moulded and engendered by Nature. Man *and* Nature, Nature *and* Mind, Matter *and* Mind, Body *and* Mind are fused into a single reality. Man as Soul or Spirit is the cosmic Person, as a body he is the non-sentient Nature. Together as world systems they are the primal 'seed' and 'womb' for all human cultures.

The existential connection between Nature and culture is explained: Elements of Nature are by themselves inert and incapable of self-movement; they move only by an extraneous agent, the Spirit. All living matter exists by the transcendent Order of Life, the one which is invisible, formless, but knowable through its effect. It renders matter the binding abilities, interlocking powers, overlapping characters and a transcendent state in which Nature is seen as a self-originating, self-organizing and self-sustaining system. Nobody knows where that Order comes from, but it is seen all around. Nature nurtures the Element. The whole process of growth and decay, order and disorder, may be seen in the rhythm of night and day, or the cycle of the seasons, and in Space and Time. At the human level, it causes bio-social types, as in the Hindu caste system (based on the principle of the genetic algorithm).

Like Elements of Nature, forms of culture are also subject to a fivefold order of origination, binding, interlocking, overlapping, and transcending. The biological Man, made of Elements, is ritually processed as a social person. The social person undergoes a transcendent (supernatural, super-psychic) process of cultivation and purification to become a cultural person. The ultimate goal of human life is transcendence, that is, the ordering of desires of earthly existence. Human desires are fourfold: desire to uphold the natural order, the desire connected with the sustenance of Life, the desire for bringing oneself into existence (by the natural process of reproduction) and the desire of transcending all desires. This approach to Life and culture is a deeply religious one. In a consciously cultivated lifestyle, directed towards the boundless dimension of Naturalness, Man as Nature is enlightened. The non-homocentric and non-technocentric view of culture takes Man as a member of the class of 'sentient being', or even as 'non-sentient being' and therefore the image of the cosmic Man. When it is said that Man has a kinship with trees and animals, the cosmological emphasis is quite conspicuous.

Drawing upon the Upanishadic imagery of the *ficus religiosa* tree, culture may be defined as an 'inverted tree' with roots in the revealed, imperishable tradition, whose stem is represented by the ritual process of transformation, whose tender leaves are the various stages of life and whose branches are the social groups nourished by action (with or without attraction and repulsion). This tree extends both downwards in earthly existence and upwards in the transcendental realm.

The true nature of human culture is imperceptible. It has neither a beginning nor an end (that is, it is ahistorical and its source is the cosmic

Intelligence), nor even stability (that is, perennial flow of tradition). Its roots are so deep-laid in transcendence that it cannot be cut by the temporal weapons of destruction (technology). From this tree has emanated a pattern of Life freed from the pairs of opposites: pleasure and pain, sacred and profane, inner and outer; and so on.

• Ritual As Language

Of all the animals, Man alone speaks a language other than his own. He communicates with birds and beasts. He also communicates with Gods, Spirits and Ancestors. He has learnt a ritual way of communication, the language of the God. Ritual is always a code which signifies a realm beyond the expression of human language. In its essential form it is a fourfold code consisting of (i) primordial Word, (ii) Gesture, (iii) Sound and (iv) everyday Language. The primordial Word used in ritual is that of which neither Man nor God is the author. It is not even the message of the God. Indeed, it is God himself. There are innumerable gestures with positions of body, hands and fingers. A gesture is sometime performed by pronouncing a primordial Word, generally for the fruition of the Word. Sound is the third constituent of the ritual language. As in outer space waves of sound are produced by movements of air, so in the space within the body waves of sound are produced according to the movements of the vital air and the process of inhalation and exhalation. Certain forms of sound are considered sacred and auspicious. There are also inauspicious sounds such as the hooting of an owl or the howling of a dog or a jackal. In all forms of chants and recitation the critical aspect is sound. The fourth constituent of the ritual code is the use of everyday language.

Ritual as a human phenomenon, displaying different dimensions of the relationship between Man and language, is universal. Since man's desire to know his place in the Universe and to overcome his existential crisis is universal, ritual language is found in all cultures. Each culture constructs its own world of the sacred. The forms of ritual language, therefore, vary from one culture to another. But the basic fourfold code suggested here is applicable to all cultures and to all kinds of religious expression. Ritual is an internal necessity; it has a function and relevance for Man because it determines his subconscious activities and is the noblest expression of his life and culture. For a man in tradition, tradition is the supreme authority.

• Tradition As Hiero-history

Tradition perceived as hiero-history refers to time in which every-time is restored to the present. Here restoration of time is not to be understood as bringing back to the original state; it means a continual renaissance. The nearest Sanskrit word for tradition is *parampara* (one after another) which signifies layers of precipitated matter accumulated in Time, as in a flood and refers to a deposit of knowledge to be nourished and to be handed down to posterity. Man is creator only in a limited sense. The basic structure of the tradition that has been revealed to him is 'unlimited in extent and unequalled in authority'. His own job is to explore, to discover and to rediscover the 'unlimited' treasure that has been handed down to him through a series of revelations. This, of course, he does in numerous ways.

The process of intellectualization of tradition is neither so simple nor so frequent as to be brought about in everyday life. Tradition-making is based on the truth-abiding principle, on the rigors of intellectual exercise. It passes through a fivefold consideration of: (i) competence, (ii) criteria of truth, (iii) fullness, (iv) compelling situation and (v) purification. Of these, the first three are procreative and the last two restorative in purpose and performance.

The norms and values of traditional society are governed by the Law of Limits to change. Tradition, by definition, is changeable. Change occurs inevitably in handing down the deposit of knowledge from one generation to the next. In a certain sense, each generation organizes its own tradition in a manner which may differ slightly or sharply from the preceding generations, as also from the generations to come. But change is brought about necessarily within certain *limits* defined by the tradition. In this manner each generation, while experiencing the present, is continuous with the past and with the future. For cultures believing in the cyclic concept of time, chronological ordering of tradition is not only unimportant but also logically inconsistent. Additions and omissions in scriptures really do not matter so long as tradition is considered in its fullness. As the sages have said, 'Fullness is taken away from fullness; yet fullness remains'.

Tradition as excellence of human organization is threefold: (i) contextualized convention, (ii) conventionalized universal and (iii) universalized transcendence. Human life is modelled by practical experience made intelligible by conventional universal experience, authenticated by the criteria of truth. Each generation contextualizes conventional experience in order to make it intelligible, recognizable and operationally viable. In time its contextualized experience becomes the conventionalized universal experience for the next generation. Backward in time are the roots of human experience — the revealed universalized transcendence — shared by every generation.

It follows then, that ordinarily at no point of time can tradition be fully realized; it can be realized only in proportion to its intelligibility. Tradition in its fullness remains timeless. But this timelessness is not to be taken as that of the pure transcendence, because it consists in a co-ordination between empirical knowledge and revelatory knowledge. It may be viewed as a certain mixture of the temporal and the transcendental reality.

• The Cosmic Anthropological Principle

The Western science of anthropology seeks to understand Man empirically by an analysis and comparison of different races and cultures. Its theory appeared to be impregnable so long as it was confined to the 'garden of simple folk'. The shift from simple to complex cultures with a high intellectual tradition has posed a big challenge. This brings us to a methodic consideration that introduces the premises on which traditional cultures stand. Modern cultures have other premises.

All traditional cultures hold that different human groups form, as it were, different life-centres originating from a cosmic condition and influencing one another in a given context of spacetime, that is, cosmology is seen as culture. Needless to say that this vision has startling implications for anthropology, particularly that of the old style which supposes that a single culture (i.e. the modern technocentric culture) can set standards for determining the state of all cultures.

Instead of elaborating the difference between the traditional and the modern premises, I would like to present a concrete example of the cosmic anthropological principle.

The key concept in the Sacred Science of Man is *brahman*, the mystery of cosmodicy. The word *brahman* has acquired a series of technical meanings, out of which has evolved the metaphysical *brahman*, in its manifold forms. It has been identified and interpreted as the potency or principle from which all things are derived, as the ultimate basis of the world, as the inner power and essence of things, as the unity of all that is named, as the form of Time and the refuge of all beings, as the fire, the wind, the lightning, the heart or the breath of life, speech, sight, hearing, understanding; and so on. With reference to the person the Mind is *brahman*, with reference to the divinities, Space. Among Gods (Brahma and others) *brahman* appeared by means of

Agni (Fire), among men as a Brahman.

Of the fourfold *varna*, the Brahman is more 'powerful' than the other three. According to *Manu*, the very birth of a Brahman is an internal incarnation of the *dharma*. The epics often repeat that 'The Brahman is the highest *tejas* (power, energy), the Brahman is the highest *tapas* (power of asceticism); it is by the honouring of Brahmans that the Sun shines in the Sky; having prowess, consisting in truth and gifted with great energy, such men, if enraged, are capable of reducing the entire kingdom to ashes; and so on'. The *varna* order was extended beyond the world of Men. Of the four kinds of soil the Brahman soil is white in colour; of the temples the Brahman form is characterized by nine divisions of the wall; of the planets, Jupiter and Venus are Brahman; of the signs of the Zodiac, Pisces, Scorpio and Taurus are Brahman. According to Indian astrology, every individual, regardless of his being a Brahman, a Kshatriya, a Vaishya or a Shudra by birth, has a *varna* of his own which is determined by the sign of the Zodiac at the time of his birth. Thus there is a chance for every individual to be a Brahman. The fourfold *varna* order pervaded also the plant and animal kingdoms. Among animals the cow is Brahman, among trees, the banyan is Brahman.

The identity of *brahman*, Brahma, and Brahman is clearly borne out by the divine precepts. The idea that Gods, humans, animals, and trees are recipients of the 'divine power' is not confined to India. Like the Indian *brahman*, the Siouan term *wakan* indicates a wonderful power with which the Universe is believed to be charged; and just like *brahman*, *wakan* may be a formula or a place or an object or a person. The Kwakiutl term *nawalak* has a very wide range of meaning (e.g. trees, the lark, the salmon, supernatural beings that manifest in visions, persons celebrating or joining religious ceremonies, etc.). The Munda term *bonga* refers to a very big power that pervades the Universe and, though being formless by itself, can assume any form. Among the Suau-Tawala (Papua) the term *gigibori* applies not only to 'power' but also to things and persons in which this 'power' resides. The Polynesian term *mana* also stands with the 'power' concept. Each of these terms or concepts has specific characteristics of its own. But the fact that *brahman* is a central concept among a large number of concepts cannot be denied. All that is connected with such a 'power-concept' can, in principle, bear the name 'cosmic hierophany'. Our cosmic hierophany (= a nearly self-sufficient partial modality of manifestation) is ruled by Death. But there are other cosmic hierophanies (= an ordered and pre-eminent modality of the plenum - the great chain of Being) which are not earth-bound. The personal and the impersonal, the animate and the inanimate, the human and the divine, the divine and the cosmic, get entirely intermingled in the manifest aspect of the potency called *brahman*.

This aspect of the cosmic hierophany is closely bound up with the solving of the anthropologists' riddle of binary opposites. The sages have described *brahman* as *coincidentia oppositorum*.

• THE ECOLOGICAL PRINCIPLE

The manifested cosmoses are spatio-temporal and have immensely long life. They are earth-bound but spiritually alive in the domain of *brahman*.

The Five Elements of our world have been perceived holistically as symbols standing for the ultimate constituent of Reality. The Elements are both material and spiritual. What binds them together is the Soul, the Inner Controller. As the *Brihadaranyaka Upanishad* says:

> He who is abiding in the Earth, yet different
> from the Earth.
> He who is abiding in the Waters, yet different
> from the Waters.
>
> He who is abiding in the Fire, yet different
> from the Fire.
> He who is abiding in the Air, yet different
> from the Air.
> He who is abiding in the Sky, yet different
> from the Sky.
> He is your Soul, the Inner Controller.

Man, whose body is made of the Elements, does not know who dwells in these Elements. The sages have said that the Earth is the Mother, the Sky is the Father; the Waters, the Fire and the Air convey the divine energy. Human existence is given over to spiritual kinship with Nature.

Man's attitude towards the planet Earth springs from his primordial experience. He is of the Earth and earthly. The Earth is his home, his own family, his body. He finds his happiness on the Earth. He discovers an intelligent pattern of understanding. The Earth is a cosmic power, the protector of all creatures. The imagery of Mother Earth is extended to a new symbol. Universal Nature or infinity has been conceived as the wish-fulfilling cosmic Cow in whose body all the divine powers abide. The Earth is her milking-pail. This Cow has four udders for streams of milk by which she supports four classes of creature: the sages, the ancestors, the Gods, and the Men. What amazing wisdom is embodied in this belief! The Earth has inexhaustible resources, enough for the survival of all.

For the sages, ecology was the Sacred Science from which they worked out a cultural formulation to realize that all Life on Earth is valuable, not just the life of *Homo sapiens*. They also made Man aware of the cosmic gift, bringing confidence and happiness to human life. Tragically, modern Man is ambivalent towards his relationship with the Earth. In Christian thinking this ambivalence has pervaded through the two thousand years of the Christian story.

Man cannot live without the Earth. At the same time, he is more than Earth. As the limb of the cosmic Man, he is mighty. As a microcosm, his body is made of cosmic Elements and his Self (Soul) is enveloped by the cosmic sheaths. From the primordial sacrifice he emerged as a ritual being. He is both a biological creature and a spiritual being: hence an autonomous being, partly free.

Man is conditioned by the Law of Life. But he is capable of the existential leap that takes him to another reality. The Buddhist theory of 'dependent origin' explains how an individual life passes through birth upon birth in the form of consciousness and how by the same chain of causation the wheel of Life stops for ever. Man's existence in the cosmic realm cannot be fully comprehended without taking into account his relationship with other beings and non-beings. The implication is that neither in *sansara* (cyclic flow of birth-death) nor in *nirvana* (cessation of rebirth) is Man alone and unique. In a general ultimate sense, he, as species, cannot attain *nirvana* until all beings and non-beings are fully enlightened. This idea is well developed in the Mahayanist tradition, which holds that animals, birds, trees, mountains, rivers and lands too attain Buddhahood. The interchange between human and cosmic is reflected further in the conception of the three kinds of body: (i) the body with human form; (ii) the body without any form or substratum, subtle and eternal and (iii) the body made of Mind. Of these, the eye of the flesh can see the human body and not the other two, which can be seen only by the Divine. The eternal body of the Buddha persists through space and time; it assumes form in various ways. Similarly, the human body can be transformed in many spiritual ways.

This is the most remarkable explanation of the relationship between the physical and spiritual dimensions of Man. In witnessing the plunder of the Earth in many countries today, the notion of Mother Earth and the cosmic Cow is not only a revelation of the self-perpetuating life process of the Earth but also a hope and message, the spiritual transformation of Man and his world.

• THE ORDERING PRINCIPLE

Traditional cultures refer to a fivefold cosmic Order that sets forth the timeless sequence of creation, preservation and dissolution. The First Order is set in zero, that is, in the beginning there was nothing. The Second Order causes primary creation of the Five cosmic Elements. The Third Order causes natural identity and differentiation in terms of colour, direction, form, smell etc. The Fourth Order causes the return to the primordial state. The Fifth Order is the Order of all orders, it repeats the scenario of the world in which everything has its proper place, and where everything grows and allows others to grow. It is inviolable.

The cosmic Order encompasses the Human Order. Traditional societies are structured on a fourfold order in terms of their social formation, subsistence, distinctions, and desires. Human groups are ordered by the three *gunas* (factors of quality), called *sattva* (light, intelligence), *rajas* (energetic, active, domineering) and *tamas* (coarse, inert, enveloping, dark). Nature is also constituted of these Factors of quality. Combining in various proportions, they make up the evolving Universe. Hence the potential differences between individuals and the objects of the Universe. In the hierarchical order, *sattva* is placed at the top, because it is luminous and contrasted with *tamas*, which is the lowest. All physical and mental phenomena are placed under the hierarchy of the Three Factors. In the human world those who possess *sattva* in abundance are called Brahman, those with *rajas* are Kshatriya, and those with *tamas* are Vaishya or Shudra.

All Orders are subjected to the Law of Numbers. The number possesses an active force. It is a symbol and its properties are sacred attributes. Like the divisions of Time, numbers are divine for a similar reason. They are said to have been revealed to mankind by the motions of the stars. They play a unique and privileged role in determining the hierarchy of infinite sets which are incomprehensible or else chaotic. The numbers are formulated in terms of cultural symbols and possibly have pre-mathematical existence. For instance, in Indian thought, *Three* signifies states of Elements, Gods, Vedas, factors of quality etc., *Four* signifies Ages, castes of Men, stages of life, kind of creation, kinds of creature, etc., *Five* signifies primordial Elements, faces of God, cosmic sheaths, classes of sages etc., *Seven* signifies seas, mountains, planets, streams of the river Ganga, divisions of the stratosphere, attendants of the Sun etc. Clearly, the number illuminates the relation of signs to meta-signs. Zero, understood as a number, assigns to the subsuming concept of the Absolute or the Ultimate; it is full and empty.

There are two forms of *brahman*: the formed and the formless, the mortal and the immortal, the stationary and the moving. Similarly, there are two types of humans: the one whose thought is individually formed is mortal and moving, the other who believes in formless is immortal and stationary. So are the two Orders of culture: the New and the Old. The New Order is formed on the premise that Man is the measure of all and hence he can create, destroy and recreate the world at his will; that human thought ought to be pursued for its own sake and that the new system of knowledge is autotelic. The Old Order maintains that the primal culture moves, and it moves not. In using the Upanishadic metaphor, it can be said that traditional cultures have historically moved in time and yet its critical intuition of understanding Reality remains unmoved.

• The Transcending Principle

There are different ways of understanding and expressing the supreme Reality. We find two definite tendencies: the tendency to stress Transcendence and the tendency to stress Immanence. A third group emerges from the combination of the two: that is of Immanent Transcendence. Emphasis on Transcendence is typical of the Semitic religions: Judaism, Christianity and Islam. The emphasis on Immanence is peculiar to the Chinese religious tradition and, curiously enough, to the modern secular spirit as well. The emphasis on the Immanent aspect of Transcendence is the characteristic of the Hindu-type religions, including 'tribal' religions.

Realities of the Immanent Transcendence are multilayered and multidimensional. Man, in the ultimate sense, is not his own principle. He is related not only to his own domain but also to what is above and below him. This is illustrated by the Hindu social system, in which the Brahman is placed at the top. The social model is derived from the cosmic model and both are hierarchical. At the transcendental level, *brahman* is the Supreme principle.

Man as microcosm transcends earthly limits through cosmic Intelligence and ritual action. Cosmogonic myths have revealed how the limits of the natural state were transcended in the beginning. The state of primordial solidarity was transcended as the cosmic Egg emerged. The Earth is limited, the Sky is unlimited. Human culture is an 'Inverted Tree', with roots upward and branches downward. As the Upanishadic sages have affirmed, Man as a citizen of the Earth and the Sky must make no difference.

> Whatever is here, that is there.
> What is there, that again is here.
> He who sees any differences here
> Goes from death to death.

Man's image of the Sky is the same as of himself, and of all that is here. The Sun, the Moon, the Stars and the seasons are the divine manifestations, each having a name, a form and an attribute of Gods, demons, humans and animals. The ancestors of Men have assumed the form of Stars. The Sun and the Moon have kinship with human beings. Man's rhythm of life is in tune with the Sky. His daily routine is organized by the cycle of the Sun; his sustenance by the cycle of the seasons; his joys (festivals) by the cycle of the Moon and so on. Like humans, the citizens of the Sky are governed by the fourfold *varna* order. In their interpersonal relationships, like humans, they are friends, enemies and neutrals. They thrive on Man's offerings and oblations.

The correspondence between Sky and Earth is not just in appearance but in operation too. The Sky and the Earth together form the cosmic rhythms of Time. Man offers sacrifice for the preservation of his own life as also of the other contingent beings. Entering into the sacrifice (the illuminant womb), Man and Time reach a state of purity and harmony - a cosmological phenomenon essential for the well-being of all. Ritual is the proper context of Man-Time interaction. It is in this context alone that Man's perception of Time can be nearer to what is true. For a man in tradition, properly speaking, there is no Time other than Ritual Time. There is no universal time covering all ritual events occurring everywhere through every individual. Ritual Time is not only discontinuous but also dependent on multiple Time orders. Ritual is observed at relative rest in due consideration of caste, age, sex and place.

Like Time, Space is of uneven quality; it is diverse and discontinuous. All places are not suitable for sacred performances, some are more sacred and effective than others. Even within sacred spaces, there are purity-space and protection-space. Ritual Time and Ritual Space are inextricably bound together. All bathing rituals and festivals are observed on special occasions in Ritual Space-Time.

Man, Time and Space are ritually constructed. Ritual is an aspect of *rita*, the cosmic Law that transcends all human laws. It causes the birth and death of all corporeal beings, things and events, and holds the cosmos by its own power. Whatever is created in Time (*kala*) dissolves naturally into the Great Time, *mahakala*. Humanly ordered Ritual Time is impermanent because a ritual act takes place in an ordinal duration of Time. But all rituals are aimed at permanence, that is, transcending the impermanence of Life. There is an essential connection between Time and Great Time; Ritual Time mediates between the two.

Ritual Act, Ritual Order and Ritual Time are inconceivable without one another. Act is realised by the virtue of Order that occurs to create a capacity to Time. Time is not an independent reality. It is set in motion by a linear continuum of Orders within which changes occur in *kairological* moments and not in a chronological order. Hence traditional cultures give no importance to lineal history. Man's quest for return to the primordial, the ultimate goal of life, is reflected in his ritual behaviour, in the archetypal creation and dissolution of Time to experience the *kairological* moment as the rhythm of Great Time.

Change is the Law of Time. Death (Great Time) causes change. It transcends Time, but nothing transcends it. In a *cosmocentric culture* Man transcends ordinal duration of Time in a ritual context that situates him in a state of perfect harmony with Nature and makes real his *experience* of transcendance. In a *technocentric culture* Man ventures to transcend Time in a temporal context; and that takes him nowhere, situates him in continual strife (direct confrontation) with Nature and makes his experience unreal.

• The One Mystery

To think of anthropology is to think of the One in which all converge and from which all issues. An anthropology that studies Man in compartments and *limits* his self-reflective procedure is not worth pursuing. The anthropological paradigms that fail to provide a sense of *wholeness* are no good. The thoughts written in this paper have ontological foundations but they show themselves more clearly in the anthropological realm. The new paradigms suggested here have a cosmic dimension and they allow themselves to dwell within one another. They reflect a deep human truth. So by virtue of logical conclusion it can be named 'The Sacred Science of Man'.

(i) 'One as Many'. The key parameter is *brahman*, the mystery of cosmodicy. Cosmologically, the expanding *brahman* pervades the whole Universe. Ontologically, it is the creating principle and at the same time that of which this worldly reality is *name-and-form.* Mathematically, it is conceived as zero which is infinite, the non-dual infinity.

(ii) 'Man as Microcosm'. Biologically, like the rest of the material world, Man is made up of the cosmic Elements: Earth, Water, Fire, Air, Sky. Metaphorically, the earthly Man is the limb of the primeval cosmic Man. The macrocosm and the microcosm are analogically One.

(iii) 'Science as Society'. Biology is connected with cosmology. The fourfoldness of Man is hieratic, not hierarchical. Man follows a complete cosmic rhythm in his social organization, subsistence strategies, interpersonal relationships and all contexts of creativity. The fourfoldness symbolizes the *wholeness* of Life.

(iv) 'Theodicy as Cosmodicy'. The *brahman* as the First Principle of the Universe does not allow raising a frontier between God, Animal and Man. All the Three are ruled by Death. This shows that all Life dwells in Death.

(v) 'Mind as Matter'. Mind is not a mere biological organism; it has created the World. Mind is formless Matter. The ancients did not draw a hard and fast line between *concreta*, e.g. a mountain and *abstracta*, e.g. energy. The First Principle of the Universe operates analogically on a variety of levels.

(vi) 'Word as World'. The Word is infinite and immense. All creatures live in the Word. This is self-evident. The World-reality is of the nature of the Word-Principle. The two interpenetrate; they are the expressed form of the Absolute.

(vii) 'Knowledge as Experience'. The key concept is *cosmic intelligence.* It can be approached by entering into the womb of the Ultimate. It has an ontological link with all beings. Human knowledge is not mere mental consciousness. Experiencing is not just knowing; it means becoming part of the experienced object. Coming into direct contact with the source of the knowable, knowledge merges with the unknowable, the Absolute.

(viii) 'Knowledge as Culture'. Culture may be defined as a deposit of knowledge accumulated in space-time. According to the modes of transmission of knowledge there are *oral, textual* and *transcendental* cultures. Based on personal factors in the development of thought, cultures are fourfold: *cosmocentric, theocentric, anthropocentric* and *technocentric.* The fourfoldness of culture goes well with the fourfoldness of human society, as also with the *wholeness* of Life.

(ix) 'Nature as Culture'. Man sees Nature as his own Self. He is moulded and engendered by Nature. Biological Man, made of the Cosmic Elements, is ritually processed as a social person. Culture is an *inverted tree* with roots in transcendence and branches in immanence. In a religiously cultivated lifestyle, directed towards the boundless dimension of naturalness, Man in Nature is enlightened. Only from Nature does Man interact directly with the whole of reality.

(x) 'Ritual as Language'. Ritual is a fourfold code consisting of the primordial word, gesture, sound and everyday language. It determines Man's subconscious activities and gives him the noblest expression of life. The fourfoldness of the ritual code bears the matrix of the fourfoldness of Man (indeed of all creation). It is ruled by the fourfoldness of Time (the four Cosmic Cycles).

(xi) 'Tradition as Hiero-history'. Tradition refers to Time in which every-time is restored to the present. Here restoration of time is not to be understood as bringing it back to its original state; it makes a continual renaissance. The Sanskrit word for tradition is *parampara*, which signifies layers of precipitated matter accumulated in Time, as in a flood and refers to the cumulative knowledge to be nourished and handed down to posterity. This permits us to grasp the reality that Man coexists with Time: the past lives in the present and the present lives in the One, which is immortal, eternal.

The Sacred Science of Man presents original premises on which all traditional cultures stand. Modern cultures have other premises. What emerges from the following premises is the concrete example of the cosmic anthropological principle.

(i) 'Cosmic Hierophany'. The *brahman* is the potency or principle from which all things are derived. It is the inner power and essence of all. With reference to the person, Mind is *brahman*, with reference to the divinities, Space. The *brahman* is identified with Brahma, the creator God and Brahman, the human incarnation of *dharma*. The idea that Gods, humans, animals and trees are recipients of the *divine power* is not confined to India. All that is connected with this 'power concept' can, in principle, bear the name 'cosmic hierophany', where the personal and the impersonal, the animate and the inanimate, the human and the divine, the divine and the cosmic, get entirely intermingled. This aspect of the cosmic hierophany is closely bound up with the solving of the anthropologist's riddle of 'binary opposites'.

(ii) 'Ecological Principle'. The manifested cosmoses are spatio-temporal and earthly. Man cannot live without the Earth. At the same time, he is more than Earth. He is conditioned by the Law of Life. At the same time he is capable of the existential leap that takes him to another reality. The notion of the living Mother Earth and the cosmic Cow reveals a self-perpetuating life-process grounded in the One.

(iii) 'Ordering Principle'. The Cosmic Order sets forth the timeless sequence of creation, preservation and dissolution and encompasses the Human Order. All traditional societies are structured in terms of social formation, subsistence, distinctions and desires. Human groups are ordered by the Three factors of quality which form a triadic whole. All physical and mental phenomena are held hierarchically by the permutations and combinations of the Three factors. All human Orders are subjected to the Law of Numbers (an active sacred force). Number is a cultural symbol that plays a unique and privileged role in determining the hierarchy of infinite sets which are incomprehensible or else chaotic. It is an aspect of cosmodicy, *rita*.

Finally, I wish to say (perhaps not alone) that there is a need to challenge ourselves, to get out of our colonial orientation, and to develop an *anthropology from within*. Must we become, intellectually, Semites if we want to be anthropologists? Must we be converted to the ways of thinking and living of one particular culture? Must we talk of global anthropology? Anthropology is not only the *logos* of Man but also the Man's *logos*: the wisdom tradition. The main emphasis has been one-sided. The 'scientific priesthood' rests on allegiance to a single culture. Every culture sets out on its journey alone and, to a great extent, remains confined or constricted by its own instruments: or else it loses its identity. But all cultures approach the One mystery, because every being participates in its cosmic *lila*, the divine play. Traditional cultures are built entirely around the concept of revelation: a non-human source of knowledge. Hence in the Sacred Science of Man, cosmology is the universal manifesting field. Its paradigms are impersonal and they belong to the family of the idea of Immanent Transcendence or Transcendent Immanence.

REFERENCES

Agrawala, Vasudeva S., 1968, *Matsya Purana: A Study*. Ramnagar-Varanasi: All India Kashiraj Trust.

Bose, N.K., 1963, *Progress of Anthropology and Archaeology*. Calcutta: Indian Science Congress Association.

Gonda, J., 1950, *Notes on Brahman*. Utrecht: J.L. Beyers.

Hume, Robert Ernest, 1984, *The Thirteen Principal Upanishads* (translated from the Sanskrit). Delhi: Oxford University Press.

Marriott, McKim, 1990, 'Constructing an Indian Ethnosociology', in *India through Hindu Categories,* McKim Marriott (ed.). New Delhi: Sage Publications.

Morris, Henry M., 1974, *Scientific Creationism*. San Diego: Creation Life Publishers.

Panikkar, Raimundo, 1977, *The Vedic Experience: Mantramanjari.* London: Darton, Longman and Todd.

——, 1979, 'Man as Ritual Being', in *Indian Theological Studies* (reprinted from *Chicago Studies* 16.1).

——, 1983, *Myth, Faith and Hermeneutics: Cross-Cultural Studies*. Bangalore: Asian Trading Corporation.

Roy, Rai Bahadur Sarat Chandra, 1938, 'An Indian Outlook on Anthropology', *Man* XXXVIIL, Nos. 171-88.

Saran, A.K., 1996, *Traditional Thought: Toward an Axiomatic Approach*. Sarnath-Varanasi: Central Institute of Higher Tibetan Studies.

Saraswati, Baidyanath, 1970, *Contributions to the Understanding of Indian Civilization*. Dharwar: Karnataka University.

——, 1977, *Brahmanic Ritual Traditions in the Crucible of Time*. Simla: Indian Institute of Advanced Study.

——, 1978, 'The Quest for Indian Tradition in Social Sciences', in *Behavioural Scientist: Essays in Honour of Professor Sachchidananda*, A.K. Lal (ed.). Patna: Bihar Council of Young Behavioural Scientists.

——, 1980, 'Man: Perspective from Indian Intellectual Tradition', in *Newsletter*. Varanasi: N.K. Bose Memorial Foundation.

——, 1982, 'Ritual Language: A Trans-anthropological Perspective', in *Man in India*, 62(1).

——, 1985, T*he Spectrum of the Sacred: Essays on the Religious Traditions of India*. New Delhi: Concept Publishing Company.

——, 1987, 'Man and Culture: The Exegeses of Science and Scripture', in *Sravanavidya Studies in Buddhism*. Sarnath-Varanasi: Central Institute of Higher Tibetan Studies.

Saraswati, Baidyanath, 1988, *Thinking About Tradition: The Indian Vision*. Varanasi: N.K. Bose Memorial Foundation.

——, 1991, 'Ritual Space: Tribal Nontribal Context', in *Concepts of Space: Ancient and Modern*, Kapila Vatsyayan (ed.). New Delhi: Indira Gandhi National Centre for the Arts.

——, 1993a, *The Sacred Science of Man*. Calcutta: Institute of Social Research and Applied Anthropology.

——, 1993b, 'Culture as Inverted Tree', in *The Contribution by Religions to the Culture of Peace*. Barcelona: UNESCO.

——, 1994, 'Animal Ontology: The Hindu Vision and Tradition', Conference paper on Animal: A Reappraisal. Toronto: Victoria University.

——, 1995, 'Cosmogonic Myths in Northeast India: Forces of Nature', in *Prakriti: The Integral Vision*, Vol. 1, Baidyanath Saraswati (ed.). New Delhi: IGNCA.

——, 1995b, 'Forms of Life in the World of Matter: Reflections on Tribal Cosmology', in *Prakriti: The Integral Vision*, Vol.4, J.V. Narlikar (ed.). New Delhi: Indira Gandhi National Centre for the Arts.

——, 1995c, 'Elements of Nature and the Order of Culture', in *Prakriti: The Integral Vision*, Vol. 5, Baidynath Saraswati (ed.). New Delhi: Indira Gandhi National Centre for the Arts.

——, 1995d, *The Sacred Science of Nature: The Verrier Elwin Memorial Lectures*. Shillong: North-Eastern Hill University.

——, 1995e, 'The Living Universe: A Unitary Vision', in *Universal Responsibility: A Felicitation Volume in Honour of HH the 14th Dalai Lama Tenzin Gyatso*, Ramesh Chandra Tiwari and Krishna Nath (eds.). New Delhi: ANB Publishers.

——, 1995f, 'Order: the Old and the New', Seminar paper on *Rita: Cosmic Order and Chaos*. New Delhi: Indira Gandhi National Centre for the Arts.

——, 1996a, 'Ritual Time: An Exegesis of Time and Great Time', in *Concepts of Time: Ancient and Modern*, Kapila Vatsyayan (ed.). New Delhi: IGNCA.

——, 1996b, 'Thinking about Culture', in *The Legacy of G.S. Ghurye*, A.R. Momin (ed.). Bombay: Popular Prakashan.

——, 1996c, 'The New Anthropology', in *The Anthropological Survey of India Golden Jubilee Celebration Lecture*. Calcutta: Anthropological Survey of India.

——, 1997a, 'Culture and Development: Guideline Questions', in *Integration of Endogenous Cultural Dimension into Development*, Baidyanath Saraswati (ed.). New Delhi: Indira Gandhi National Centre for the Arts.

——, 1997b, 'Orality and the Complexity', Seminar paper on *Katha Vachana aur Katha Vachak: Exploring India's Chanted Narratives*. New Delhi: Indira Gandhi National Centre for the Arts.

——, 1997c, 'Nature as Culture: The Vision of a Tradition', Seminar paper on *Santhal World View*. New Delhi: Indira Gandhi National Centre for the Arts.

Saraswati, Baidyanath, 1998, 'Mind the Elephant: A Sacred Science View of Reality', Seminar paper on *Mind, Man and Mask*. New Delhi: Indira Gandhi National Centre for the Arts.

Vatsyayan, Kapila, 1993, 'Indian Art: The One and the Many', *The Jawaharlal Nehru Memorial Lecture*. London: The Nehru Centre.

——, 1999, 'Thinking about Sound in Traditional Sciences', in *Dhvani: Nature and Culture of Sound*, S.C. Malik (ed.). New Delhi: Indira Gandhi National Centre for the Arts.

Vaudeville, Ch., 1974, *Kabir*, Vol. 1. Oxford University Press.

Williams, Robert Charles, 1983, 'Scientific Creationism: An Exegesis for a Religious Doctrine', in *American Anthropologist* 85.

2

VIEWS ON MAN AND HIS NATURE IN INDIAN PHILOSOPHY

Makhan Jha

Anthropos and *logus*, i.e., the science of man, developed in the West, are not adequately equipped to explain the concept of man and his nature as explained and discussed in the Indian classical texts. Man (*purusha*) becomes the *de facto* empirical creation of the de-spiritualized Nature (*prakriti*), which is constituted of three factors of quality (*guna*): *sattva, rajas* and *tamas*. In their mutual relation and in varying preponderance of the one over the other, the three *gunas* determine the structure, quality and function of all existence — physical, biotic and psychical. The human individual is no exception to this general law of the creative operation of *prakriti*. Human nature, as discussed in India's sacred texts — in all its richness and variety, in its heights and its depth, in its psycho-physical expansion, and its spiritual transcendence along its vertical plane — is at once an attractive and a baffling study. Many Indian texts, like the *Sankhya* philosophy, the *poorba* and *uttar-Mimamsa* texts, the *Upanishads*, the *Yogavasistha*, the *Charak Samhita*, the *Bhagvat Gita*, and various Buddhist and Jain literature, attempt to classify man and his nature.

In this paper, an attempt is made to discuss some of the critical aspects of man and his nature.

• Human Nature

There are two distinguishable aspects of human nature. One, the aspect of uniqueness that makes every man to be himself and nobody else; and the other, the aspect of commonness and shareability which supplies the basis of classification for the sciences. Human nature in itself is an integral whole in which these two aspects act and react upon each other. The aspect of uniqueness seems to be as yet beyond analysis.

The *Sankhya* system of philosophy emphasizes on the pragmatic universe. The *Maya* of the Upanishadic tradition, which regards it a conscious universal force of *atman*, is metamorphosed into an unconscious universal reality, and its creative agency is not only retained but also made absolute.

The *Yogavasistha*, in conformity with the *Sankhya*, lays down that the core of human personality is consciousness (*chitta*) whose real pivot is desire. The importance of desire (*vasana*), as the *swarupa* (real nature) of *chitta* has its Vedic corroboration. It has been said that desire (*kama*) existed from the very first day of existence as the seed of mind (*manas*). The same pivotal character of activity is emphasized in the *Sankhya* scheme of evolution where the intellect (*buddhi*) evolves into ego (*ahankara*) in which *rajas* predominates and this leads later on to subject-object differentiation. The desire of the individual then directs the intellect to know its object and knowledge into action. However, in modern psychological expression desire is the will-to-live, irrespective of differences of opinion between Jung and Freud.

Most writers are not so particular about explaining the varieties of physical structure in human beings; they are chiefly concerned with distinguishing their temperamental diversities. The *Dharmashastra* has given a psycho-sociological scheme of classification in order to establish the fourfold social structure (*chaturvarna*) defined on the basis of mental qualities and abilities of man exhibited under the general influence of *sattva, rajas* and *tamas* and the distinctive influence of the *svadharma* of each class. Division of labour, based on the principle of *svadharma*, thus developed, rendered the classification apparently stereotyped and yet it has a value of its own; it was based on the view that the laws of *karma* and heredity were the great determining factors in the development of human nature.

Astrology has developed distinguishable human types in the light of the various traits of characters as existed under planetary influence and the signs on human palms, feet and foreheads, which, they claim, play a significant role in determining the character of man. Individual human beings, like all other entities of the world, are never isolated phenomena, but are always related to the cosmic whole, whose forces are pooled together to make them what they are.

Charak, the expounder of the Ayurvedic system of medicine, has analysed the human constitution as a mind-body complex with a view to discovering bodily and mental diseases and their remedies. He has noted that psycho-biological materials help in scientific understanding and classification of human nature.

Charak claims that diseases, both physical and mental, can be established by the consideration of the influences of the three *gunas (sattva, rajas* and *tamas)*, coupled with the humoral influences resulting from the undue preponderance of one or the other of the three humours of *vayu* (wind), *pitta* (bile) and *kapha* or *slesman* (phlegm). The ancient doctors, including Charak, have given us the key in therapeutics regarding restored natural condition of identity, deviation from which is equivalent to disease. Disease is called *Vikara* or *anatmyata*, that is, a state in which a man is other than his own being. To cure a being is to restore its true normal self. This applies equally to cases of physical and psychical pathology.

Charak made a classification of human nature named after some of the principal gods and demi-gods, taking into consideration the qualities of three *gunas*.

(A) On The Basis Of Sattva Guna

With reference to divine entity :

1. Brahma-sattva

Highly intellectual and moral, capable of scientific, philosophical and religious discourses, not overpowered by emotions and lower impulse, truthful, having restraint over the senses and impartial to all beings.

2. Arya-sattva

Endowed with keen perception, with power of persuasion and of understanding scientific truth, given to performance of religious rites enjoined by the texts, hospitable to guests, restrained in senses, and not overpowered by emotions and impulses.

3. Aindra-sattva

Energetic, powerful, unfatigued by activities, endowed with foresights and with powerful speech and given to religious, economic and pleasure-giving activities.

4. Yama-sattva

Having regard for secular duties endowed with presence of mind, indomitable in pursuits, endowed with strong memory and unaffected by lower impulses and emotions.

5. Varuna-sattva

Calm, but courageous, abhorrent of the unclean, fond of aquatic pastimes, unfatigued in strains, discriminate in the show of anger and resentment and giving patronage to the deserving.

6. KUBERA-SATTVA

Fond of family life, given to the performance of religious and secular duties, indiscriminate in the show of pride and pleasure and favouring and chastising fellow beings according to their merits and demerits.

7. GANDHARVA-SATTVA

Fond of music and dancing, interested in stories, histories and *Puranas*, having an affinity for scents, flowers and cosmetics and fond of the company of women.

(B) ON THE BASIS OF RAJAS GUNA

With reference to demoniac and aggressive animal species :

1. ASUR-SATTVA

Characterized by physical prowess, furiousness, self-conceit, love of money, etc.

2. RAKSHAS-SATTVA

Marked by ending wrath, aggressiveness; cruelty, fond of eating (specially flesh), malicious, hardy and sleep-loving.

3. PISACH-SATTVA

Indolent, unclean, cowardly, intimidating and sensual.

4. SARPA-SATTVA

Heroic in anger but cowardly in other moods, expert in counsels, strong in habits and given to the pleasures of the senses.

5. PRAITYA-SATTVA

Loving food, unpleasant by nature and in conduct in dealing with others, pained at other's prosperity, greedy and lethargic.

6. SAKUNA-SATTVA

Given to sensuous desires, gluttonous, fickle, ruthless and extravagant.

(C) ON THE BASIS OF TAMAS GUNA

Named after animals and vegetation :

1. PASAVA-SATTVA

Dirty in dress, ignoble in dealings, given to eating, drinking and sensuality, sleepy and prone to rejection of everything.

2. MATSYA-SATTVA

Cowardly, stupid, gluttonous, fickle, given to anger and sensuality and fond of travel and of water.

3. VANASPATYA-SATTVA

Living purely a vegetative life, inactive, food-seeking and totally devoid of intellectual activities.

Besides these types of human nature, as explained by Charak, the human nature is also explained in some of the religious texts, Hindu, Buddhist and Jain literature.

The *Bhagavad-Gita* has made a classification of human nature. Answering to the main faculties of the human mind (thinking, feeling, will, knowledge, desertion and action), three ways (*margas*) of life have been conceived. These three *margas* are not open to all, though they are not antagonistic to one another. Human nature, as it pursues with emphasis on one or other of these three, falls into three classes. The individual, on whom prevails the elements of *karma-marga*, is called the *karma-yogi*. The *bhakta yogi* is one who pursues the *bhakta-marga*, the path of devotion. The *gyan-marga* or the path of contemplation is adopted by the *gyan-yogi*. In each case, what is essentially required is the purging or purification of one's being by proper acquisition and retention of the influence of the element of *sattva*, followed by the gradual elimination of the influences of the elements of *rajas* and *tamas*.

There are stages in the process of spiritual elevation corresponding to the varieties of human nature. By avoiding untruth, anger, aggression, greed and similar other negative qualities, one possesses the *daivi sampada* (divine treasure). Those who are given to pride and anger, egoism and ignorance and similar, other spiritual depravities, are known as the holders of the *asuri-sampada* (demoniac treasure). The *Gita* attempts another classification of man's nature according to his *shraddha* (preponderant desire) — *sattviki, rajasi* and *tamasiki* — resulting from the dominating influence of the fundamental constitutional components of *sattva, rajasi* and *tamas* on his life's desire. A man is what he is according to his desire.

In the Buddhist literature too, attempts at classification of men and women have been made from the ethical and religious points of view. The *puggala-pannathi*, the Dhatukatha and the Dhammasangani, which form parts of the *Abhidhamma Pitaka*, contain valuable classification of human nature.

The Jains, who have developed an independent system of ethical personalism, also formulated a scheme of classification of human nature. The *jiwa* (life), according to them, is subject to the influence of *karmic* matter, which affects its originally pure nature in various degrees. The soul of the *jiwas*, though originally pure, becomes contaminated by what the Jains call *yoga* and *kasaya*, i.e. vibration of matter and passion that tinges the soul. The immediate consequence of these two forces is to generate what the Jains style *lesya* (emotion), bad or good. They have been realistically associated with six colours — black, blue or indigo, grey, yellow, red and white. These six kinds of *lesyas* supply us with a classification of human nature in an ascending scale of ethical perfection. The man belonging to good *lesya* is freed from all contamination and is on the way to *moksha* (salvation).

To conclude, the ancient Indian texts have thrown light on the nature of man in a wider perspective, irrespective of any ethnic consideration. As a matter of fact, human nature is much more complex than what modern scientists have observed. Anthropologists have not yet given sufficient attention to India's ancient texts, highlighting human nature. Textual anthropology or literary anthropology can provide a comprehensive classification of Man and his nature.

REFERENCES

Bhattacharya, Hari Mohan, 1953, 'Types of Human Nature', in *Cultural Heritage of India*, Vol. III. Calcutta: Ramkrishan Mission Institute of Culture.

Jha, Makhan, 1995, *An Introduction to Indian Anthropology.* New Delhi: Vikas Publications.

——, 1997, *Man and Society.* New Delhi: Inter-India Publications.

Kosambi, D.D., 1962, *Myths and Reality*, Bombay: Portland Prakashan.

Kane, P.V., 1930, *History of Dharmashastra.* Pune: Bhandarkar Oriental Research Institute.

Nivedita and Anand Coomarswami, 1914, *Myths of the Hindus and Buddhists.* London: George G. Harrapa & Co.

Ray, S. Sibha, 1928, *Srimad Bhagavata Puranam.* Tirupati.

3

CONCEPT OF SELF IN INDIAN CULTURE

N.K. Behura

• Introduction

The empirical approach in social and cultural anthropology somewhat follows the line of natural history. In this enterprise social and cultural anthropology differs from allied social sciences. Barth (1979:16) writes that 'Anthropologists tend to seek the strange and the exotic, approaching such matters with the naturalist's curiosity. The effect of such an approach is that one exposes oneself to the greatest possible variety and mass impressions. The immediate purpose of this is, of course, to collect and cross-check information. But it also colours the anthropologist's theoretical orientation by encouraging eclectic model building; the anthropologist is concerned about the direct relevance of theories to empirical facts, because of his constant need to order a diversity of such facts. This does not mean that, temperamentally, many social anthropologists may not wish to protect their orthodoxy from uncongenial facts, or to work deductively from a basic theory of society'. But when an anthropologist conducts his/her fieldwork in an alien society certainly he is surrounded by strangeness and thus is prone to misconstrue the socio-cultural reality.

This incongruence can be resolved and unity of the micro and macro level can be achieved by laying relatively more emphasis on emic point of view. This will help the anthropologist to map the shared cognitive categories and gross values of the informants as participating actors in the socio-cultural system. However, there are possibilities of getting two categories of data, which are complementary to each other rather than being contradictory. One category of data may conform to stable structural features and the other account for change. It is needless to say that data relating to both persistence and change are essential. In the fieldwork situation the anthropologist may be confronted with certain paradoxes. In order to overcome this he/she will have to grasp and comprehend the nature of data and separate those that pertain to stability and order from those that account for dynamism and change. It behoves that the anthropologist will have to bear in mind that he/she will have to build dynamic models so as to explain his/her social facts. In view of this necessity he/she will have to make a distinction between 'historical' and 'structural' time (Barth, 1979:24).

Barth states that in order to achieve this 'We need to process our direct impressions so as to transform and categorize them in a way that makes them into data' (1979: 25). This process involves the following exercises: (i) aggregation from single items to patterns of expectations or obligations in a social system or frequencies of behavioural forms; (ii) interpretation and elucidation of the objective meaning of social actions and (iii) securing 'bridgeheads' with foreign cultures through the application of the technique of effective participant observation.

It is essential for social and cultural anthropologists to build models for organizing and explaining socio-cultural facts. But in view of the kind of data they deal with it is not possible for them to construct such scientific models which natural scientists build. From this viewpoint social and cultural anthropology is a nascent science, which some even term as a 'Primitive' science.

Anthropologists continue to study social systems and cultures mainly depending on 'interviews' and 'observation' of actions in natural situations. But they 'cannot adequately represent, much less understand, the forms of regularity except with reference to their underlying determinants and this entails the need to map out the culture, the actor's own categories and meanings, to depict the social system' (Barth, 1979: 30). For depicting the social order the anthropologist will have to concentrate either on the 'system of jural rules' (basic ideas about interpersonal obligations and rights embodied in a culture) or the 'system of cognitive categories' (the manner in which the members of a society conceptualize and order their own social status and groups) or the 'interactional system' (the customs that constrain individual behaviour which arises from the behaviour of others in a social system).

• Concept Of Person In Hindu India

In the Indian context an individual is a *vyakti* or person. He/she is part of the hierarchical collectivist social system, yet he/she has certain functional autonomy. Indian social system (the Hindu) shapes and promotes a type of personhood which is compatible with its hierarchical collectivist holistic ethos. A 'person is also conceived as an individual, ontologically prior to any collectivity and containing within himself all the attributes of humanity' (Carter, 1982: 119). Society as a whole is regarded, in principle, as a 'collection of individuals' and a 'collective individual' (Dumont, 1971: 33). This is said to be not true of the Indian social system where hierarchical opposition of the pure and impure is ontologically prior to any empirical person (Carter, *op.cit*). It means that persons are regarded as possessing different and unequal cultural attributes. Simultaneously it is also not true that they do not share or are associated with any normative principle. The Indian social system stresses both holistic perspective as well as individualism or personhood.

• Concept Of Person And Social Group In Orissa

A *vyakti* or individual self is an element or unit in the interrelationship of a social whole, that may be the *parivar* or elementary family, *kutumba* or extended family, *jnatibhai* or lineage members, *gotra* or descent group and *jati* or caste. A *vyakti* is a multiplex of statuses, who enacts roles thereof in interactional situations as per their appropriateness. A *shishu* or child is not a *vyakti*, because it is still in the process of nourishment and primary enculturation. A *vyakti* at the same time is a member of several hierarchic social groups. The term *vyakti* does not connote any specific gender; it stands for both male and female alike. And further, it also does not refer to any specific position in the social structure. It refers to an unspecified or anonymous person in the society. It is third person singular and its corresponding plural term is *vyaktigana* (or *janamanas*), meaning sapient humans. While enquiring about the identity of a third person one may ask: *se vyakti kiye*? (who is that person?) or *se manas kiye*? (who is that human?). Similarly, while making specific enquiries about a man or woman one asks: *se bhai/puo/loka/athithi kiye*? (who is that brother/son/man/guest?) or *se bhauni/jhia/mahila/athithi kiye?* (who is that sister/daughter/lady/guest?).

The term *prani* refers to any human, male, female, young and old. People refer to a married couple in unnamed manner as *se dui prani* (those two living beings). Animals are distinguished from humans by being referred to as *itara prani* (inferior living beings). Animals have been relegated to the status of inferior life – form by the low virtue of their *karma* (deed) in their previous *jeevan* (life). They, by their *kukarma* (undesirable deed) have morally forfeited humanhood. The Hindu ideology amply makes it clear that in the life process an individual may attain sublimity through meritorious action and take *punarjanma* (rebirth) in a *ucchajati* (higher caste) and *sukhiparivar* (happy family). On the contrary if a person lives an *apakarma jeevan* (debased life) he/she may be reborn as a human in a *neechajati* (lower caste) to lead a *prapiditajeevan* (painful life or life of suffering). In the cultural context *karma* (deed) and *prakriya* (social interaction) though are governed by social rules, yet are individual centric. Individual actors have the freedom to vary their actions; they are not fully merged or fused in the social whole as Dumont claims (1970: 9). Individual cultural autonomy in the pursuit of individual happiness is seldom fully sacrificed in the caste-based Indian social system. Indians in their social system are not social automatons and conduct their social transactions most often in their self-interest and sometimes in socially desirable manner too. In role playing such values of 'individualism' as 'equality' and 'liberty' are tolerated in the society. It is the question of interpretation of the ideology by the social scientists. The hallmark of the ideology of Indian social system is not only 'hierarchy', but 'equality' too. The assumption that the criteria of 'purity and pollution' are the determinants of the structure of various sub-groups and groups of the Indian social system is not empirically tenable. For instance, the hierarchic relationship within the structure of family, lineage and descent group is not based on the dual principle of ritual purity and pollution.

Individual happiness and the autonomy are never fully sacrificed although one conforms to the norms of the collective whole. Individual liberty is never fully surrendered to the castes and families as Mines claims (1988: 79). And again the claim that equality is displaced by hierarchy as the principle structuring social relationships within particular groups is not correct and is misleading. The principle may hold good as regards structuring of social relationships among the castes. Schneider (1968) and other Western scholars, who deny existence of individualism in Indian society, totally misrepresent empirical facts. They assert that in the Indian context a person is a composite of transferable particles that form personal substance. The concept that 'the person... can improve personal substance and thus rank by regulating exchanges or transactions or transactions that involve a transmission of substance particles' (Marriott and Inden, 1977) is equally erroneous. Indian society recognizes merit and provides equality of opportunity for demonstration of merit, which is an accepted value.

Erikson's (1979: 25) assertion that the Indian social structure does not permit the emergence of a cogent adult role as perceived in Western societies and one's individual needs are subordinated to the 'interest of the group, be it a family, a kinship group, a clan or a class is upheld as virtue' is partly correct and it is not the total truth. Every member of the Indian society is aware of self versus group interest and though they skilfully shuttle between the two their goal is to maximise self-interest.

Mines regards Kakar's analysis of *ashrama dharma* as more ideological and normative than behavioural. He writes that 'Indians do imagine the possibility of autonomy and independence, just as they also recognize fusion' of life and salvation (1985: 82). But he seems to be ignoring the fact that ideology is of prime importance because it guides action. However, there is the need for separation of the mundane from the textual for understanding the autonomous self-interest of person-hood or self. Within the framework of ideology, individualism operates which in course of time brings in change in the established ideology.

• Social Dynamics And Person-hood

Explanations about self or person-hood in Indian society, which centre around caste hierarchy, social status and ritual purity and pollution to the exclusion of other features of self-identity and motivation are erroneous. According to the scheme of *grihasth ashrama* or *ashrama dharma*, life of a person is divided into four stages : (i) *brahmacharya* or celibacy, (ii) *garhasthya* or householder, (iii) *vanaprastha* or hermitage and (iv) *sanyasa* or renunciation (monasticism). The phase of *brahmacharya* is of austerity, discipline, inculcation and learning. During this phase one is dependent on his/her parents, family, household and kins for comprehensive support and sustenance. One thus remains confirmed to group norms and values. The hallmark of this phase of life comprises gross obedience, subservience, docility and acceptance of set patterns unquestionably. The stage of *garhasthya* is the most vital one in one's life as one assumes worldly responsibilities and participates in the decision-making process. A person moves to a position of superordination from that of subordination. During this stage several persons, specifically the influential ones, become promoters of self-interest, either tacitly or openly. They endeavour to realize personal goals in disregard to group goals. Sometimes they project personal goals perceptively as group goals. The strong motivation for this is attainment of greater socio-economic self-interest, even though it may run counter to the goals of the encompassing social groups. It is commonplace knowledge that in Hindu joint families the head of household often makes wasteful investment on his unworthy sons. Simultaneously he avoids promotion of educational interest of children of other members of the joint family under some pretext or the other. If concealed attempt is made to contain the activities of such independent minded persons, they become rebellious against the encompassing group and forcefully effect change in the existing system.

After the transition from the *brahmacharya* (adolescent stage) to *garhasthya* (adulthood), both men and women, assume sex-linked and non-sex-linked, traditional or non-traditional and private or public occupations. Once they are engaged in gainful and productive activities they realize their economic independence and adventurous persons flout cultural and social structural dictates. They explain their non-conformity as the desirable goal in the context of changing times. According to the views of progressive individuals, healthy competition is a desirable phenomenon. It can ensure social progress. They denounce 'hierarchical collectivist' model of society as degenerative and retrograde. The pace of this change has been accelerated during the last five decades as the modern secular-democratic polity encourages such change.

- Criteria Of Person-hood

Like ancient and scriptural division of life into four successive stages, in modern times too the life of an individual in the socio-cultural context is punctuated into four phases, such as, *balyavastha* (childhood), *jauvanavastha* (youth), *praudhavastha* (adulthood) and *bardhakya* (old age). Similar to the *garhasthya* stage, *praudhavastha* or the adulthood is the most important one in the flow of socio-cultural life. This is because the *praudha* or adult is considered as *paripakwa* or matured, *budhivanta* or intelligent and *vicharvanta* or having capacity for judgement. Therefore, they assume, as per tradition, command of the society. Obviously the more intelligent and capable individuals amongst them appropriate to themselves the social decision-making process either manifestly or latently and steer the process of social change.

Earlier reference has been made to the concept of *vyakti*. It implicitly refers to an adult person of any gender though explicitly it refers to all *jeevita* (living) humans. It alludes to adults because it is they who dominate the social scenario and are in control of system-sustaining *samajika kamakarya* (social activities). In contrast to the adults, children and adolescents are in the process of growing up, learning social norms and gradually getting adjusted to the *samajika pratha* (social system). Likewise, the old are in the process of decline and withdrawal and therefore, they are dependents. They individually await for their *prasthana* (departure) from the *mayasamsar* (mystic world). During the stage of *bardhakya* (old age) one invariably passes through the results of one's *karma* (deeds). This is notwithstanding the belief in the aftermath of life of the soul. The *karma*, which he/she has performed after becoming mature, specifically during adulthood, when all the *guna* (qualities) of a person are at their peak, are said to be causative factors for the enjoyments or sufferings in the old age. *Manav sharira* (human body) is *mara* (perishable) but *atma* (soul) is *amara* (imperishable). *Deha or sharira* (body) is referred to as *sthulasharira*, or gross material body and *atma* is termed as *sukshmasharira* or ethereal body of a *jeeva* (creature). *Sharira* is the seat of *atman*. Both *sharira* (body) and *atman* (soul) are brought into action in *karma* or deed. Both *sharira* (body) and *atman* (soul) are believed to be fully matured and fit during adulthood. Therefore, a person is adjudged or evaluated on the basis of his *karma* or deeds, which he/she has performed during adulthood.

According to Hindu Cosmology all emerging matters in the world, including humans, possess three vital *guna* (qualities) such as *sattva* (illumination/truth), *rajas* (energy/passion) and *tamas* (darkness/inertness). The emergence of all forms of subtle and gross matter is to be found in the three classes of *guna*: *sattva*, *raja* and *tamas*. 'The bodies of living creatures differ not only in being based upon different qualities but rather in being based upon different balances among the same qualities. Thus, in human beings the *sattva* and *rajagunas* are dominant, while in animals the *raja* and *tamagunas* and in plants *tamagunas* are dominant (Carter, 1983:122). When these *gunas* are in a state of equilibrium there is no further intellectual movement or evolution. Various combinations of these *gunas* take place in varying degrees of predominance within *prakriti* (primordial principles of matter). *Prakriti* has an inherent teleology which sometimes disturbs the equilibrium and various combinations of *gunas* take place. All human beings though are capable of making moral judgements, their capacities to do so grossly vary, because their *buddhi* (intellect) is not at par. This proves that all persons are not equal and this inequality is recognized in the society.

The Hindu concept of the duality of *sthulasharira* (body) and *sukshmasharira* (soul) or *atman* poses a philosophical problem. On death of a person, the body disappears once for all but the soul, as per the belief pattern, persists and moves from birth to birth depending on the merit of action one has performed. The state of *karma* is supposed to have been assessed by the Almighty.

It is believed that the pattern of life of persons has been predetermined. A horoscope is prepared for every person on the basis of planetary positions at the time of birth. Planetary positions in the zodiac provide an explanatory indication about the fate and nature of the person concerned. It is said that on the basis of the position of astral bodies as many as 211 types of horoscopes are possible and each stands for a specific type of person on the basis of planetary combinations. Members of a given society or community with a given way of life vary amongst themselves because they are born on different dates and at different times and are influenced by varying planetary positional combinations.

People assert that a person's *vyaktitva* (personality) though is shaped by his/her family, society and culture, it is imperceptively influenced by the preordained divine force as laid down in his/her fate and one's horoscope bears irrevocable testimony to that. It is believed that *atma* (soul) in the *sharira* (body), which is part of *paramatma* (divine soul), provides life and *karma* (action or deed) is the function of *sharira* (body and *manas* (mind). Human souls are in essence, possessed of omniscience and omnipotence, but such powers are obstructed, by the accumulated coverings on them on account of their inherited *karmas* (deeds) from previous lives. People in general are engaged in *sakamakarma* or work for some material object. While doing so some follow the norms laid down by the society and some others manipulate them to their advantage.

The theory of *karma* and transmigration of souls plays a prominent and fundamental role in the life of people in village communities. Any action – good, bad or natural, yields its corresponding results. The joys and sorrows of humans in the present life are predestined and predetermined by the nature of *karma* performed in a previous birth. Desire, thought and physical action, mutually interlinked, form the three strands which are twisted into the cord of *karma*. Although *karma* plays a vital part in determining the life here, humans are provided with freedom and opportunity to better their lives here by doing good deeds for which they have been bestowed with the power of discrimination. It is maintained that this has an ethical value as it provides them an incentive to overcome fatalism by undertaking good deeds.

It is believed that the *karma* of a previous birth seeks out its appropriate doer in this birth to yield the corresponding fruit. Those with gentle nature are rewarded in several ways and the cruel and heartless are punished in the same community or society. Reward encourages morality and discourages immorality. In a community all are not on the same ethical plane hence they are unequals and maintain their respective individualism.

• Concept Of Self

The concept of 'self' is a cultural construct in Indian society, which continues to be overwhelmingly traditional. In empirical life 'subject' and 'object', the self and the non-self, are radically opposed to each other. People, while describing their body, senses and mind differentiate the 'self' from 'non-self'. People consciously do not confound 'self' with 'non-self' or 'ego' with Almighty. The concept of 'self' is dynamic in the *jeevan-chakra* (life cycle). 'Self' has its constituent elements, some of which are central and some others are peripheral. The central elements constitute the governing property of a particular 'self', which account for its identity. The central constituent elements of a 'self' remain constant, whereas peripheral elements do change. For instance, sex and parentage of a 'self' are unalterable. 'Self' is conscious in all socio-cultural interactions and transactions and thereby each self maintains its distinctive identity. It does so through the canvas of socio-cultural reality. Knowledge is not an attribute of the self, but superimposition on it. The self or *atman* is of the nature of pure consciousness. Such consciousness is to be equated with pure *jnana* or knowledge. The *atman* in itself is the substrate and substance of such *jnana*. It is *jnana svarupa* or embodiment of knowledge. In other words, as in Vedantic philosophy, the whole world of mental creation emanates from and returns to Supreme self or *atman*. Thus *atman* is not to be confused with individual self.

Each self is a structural element in the social milieu through the manifestation of different statuses. Selves are composed of ephemeral elements, like body, mind and senses. Whereas a self emerges through the *atman* or soul, which is immutable and indestructible, human self functions through *sharira* (body), *manas* (mind), *buddhi* (intellect) and *ahankara* (ego), which are objects of knowledge, are variable and therefore, not the *atman*. Some Western scholars transfer the essence and qualities of self to *atman* in order to identify the former with the latter. However, the *atman* is the subject, when one studies the social behaviour of an individual.

In Indian thought *atman* refers to the non-self and is identified with the *brahman*, which is essentially *nirguna* (without any attribute), *niskriya* (without any activity or movement), *nir-avayava* (without any parts), *nir-upadhika* (unconditioned and absolute) and nirvisesa (having no distinguishing element in it). It is pure being, pure consciousness and pure blendedness. Humans are just the reverse of this. The world is always in a state of flux.

In the Upanishads there are two interrelated currents of thought about Reality, namely *saprapancha* (cosmic) and the *nisprapancha* (acosmic). According to the first view, the *brahman* is the source of manifestation of the universe; and according to the second, the world has an illusory and transient appearance. The cosmic view of Reality is that the Real is one substance out of which the many modes constituting the world have come forth, thus the *brahman* is *saguna* as the creator, the bearer of the attributes. The acosmic view, on the other hand, regards the *brahman* as the Supreme Self or the Absolute as the indistinct substratum whereon the illusory world show appears, *brahman per se is nirguna*, attributeless. The Supreme is at once transcendental, the cosmic, the social and individual reality.

The whole cosmos is set forth mainly in a negative form, showing thereby that our empirical categories and limiting concepts do not explain phenomena correctly. The cultural image of self in Indian society needs to be dealt with taking into consideration the empirical reality as well as the scriptural viewpoint. The views of Dumont (1970: 8), Marriott and Inden (1977: 232), Erikson (1979: 25), Barnett (1976: 149) and others that individualism is devalued in Indian society is not correct. It is true that Indian social system, by and large, is influenced by caste system, but it is not correct to say that personal autonomy is subordinated to collectivism always. Social demands, personal interests and cultural interpretations are not uniform in all the stages of the life of an individual. During adulthood individualism grows stronger as individuals, both men and women, feel free and become more assertive.

In the old age most Indians become scripture oriented and follow the popular path of scriptural prescriptions. Therefore, postulates of Western social scientists about 'person' in Indian society are not correct when scrutinised within the dual framework of empiricism and scriptural view point. Scriptures provide the basis for socio-cultural ideology for Indian population. Sankara developed the transcendental approach to the problem of reality as was suggested by the Upanishads and believed that this alone held the key to a metaphysical position that would avoid the shortcomings of substantialism on the one hand and those of the theory of universal becoming on the other. The *atman* is therefore, neither a substance underlying the changing states of consciousness, nor is it a mere stream of consciousness. It is indefinable yet *svayamsiddha* and *svaprakasha* principle, or an eternal conscious principle in which existence is knowledge and knowledge is existence. Objective principles of space, time and causality are applicable in a dynamic frame (Bhattacharya, 1983: 498).

Every human is born to a society and its processes influence the behavioural pattern of its members. The relationship of a human self with his/her cultural heritage is very intimate. Though the social self is reflected in the self of every individual member, yet each man or woman exhibits some unique features. Thus, in Indian society humans are humans and do assert personal independence and freedom.

REFERENCES

Barnett, S., 1976, 'Coconuts and Gold: Relations Identity in a South Indian Caste', in *Contributions to Indian Sociology*, 10:133-56.

Barnett, S., L. Fruzetti and A. Ostor, 1976, 'Hierarchy Purified', in *Journal of Asian Studies* 35:627-46.

Bhattacharya, H., 1983, *Cultural Heritage of India*, Vol. IV. Calcutta: The Ramakrishna Mission Institute of Culture.

Carter, A.T., 1983, 'Hierarchy and the Concept of Person in Western India', in *Concept of Person— Kinship, Caste and Marriage in India*. A. Ostor, L. Fruzetti and S. Barnett (eds.). Delhi: Oxford University Press.

Dumont, L., 1970, *Homo Hierarchicus : The Caste System and its Implications*. Chicago: University of Chicago Press.

——, 1983, *Affinity and Value*. Chicago: University of Chicago Press.

Inden, R., 1986, 'Orientalist Constructions of India', in *Modern Asian Studies* 20(3):401-46.

Marriott, M. and R. Inden, 1977, 'Toward an Ethnosociology of South Asian Caste System', in *The New Wind: Changing Identities in South Asia*, Kenneth David (ed.). The Hague: Mouton.

Mines, M., 1981, 'Indian Transitions: A Comparative Analysis of Adult Stage of Developments', *Ethos*, 9:95-121.

——, 1988, 'Conceptualizing the Person: Hierarchical Society and Individual Autonomy in India', *South Asian Social Scientist*. 4:77-96.

Ostor, A., L. Fruzetti and S. Barnett (eds.), 1983, *Concepts of Person — Kinship, Caste and Marriage in India*. Delhi: Oxford University Press.Introduction

4

PHILOSOPHICAL ANTHROPOLOGY IN THE DISCOURSE OF SUFISM

A.R. Momin

Contemporary western anthropology is faced with a virtual *cul de sac*. The crisis in the discipline has been precipitated by a set of three factors. For one thing, the conventional subject matter of the discipline, namely the small scale preliterate societies of the non-Western world, has almost disappeared, leaving a good many Western anthropologists in a state of confusion and disarray (Diamond, 1981).

Secondly, the traditional view of anthropology as being concerned with the 'otherness' of 'other people' (Beattie, 1964; Leach, 1982) has become debatable and contentious. A devastating criticism of this colonial definition of the discipline has been mounted by what has come to be known as indigenous anthropology in the Third World. In the process, the fallacies and misapprehensions of Western anthropologists about the study of one's own society have been laid to rest (Srinivas, 1966; Fahim, 1980; Momin, 1984). Thirdly, the disenchantment with the natural science model, especially among the senior practitioners of the discipline, has been greatly accentuated in recent years (Geertz, 1983; Jarvie, 1984; Berreman, 1981). There is an increasing realisation of the fact that the thoughtless importation of the Cartesian-Newtonian world-view and scientific methodology in the human sciences has produced a fragmentary and reductionistic picture of human nature and society. Consequently, there has come about a much-needed soul-searching and self-introspection about the self-definition and identity of anthropology.

The crisis faced by anthropology should be viewed in the wider context of the radical reorientation of thought that has taken place in the Western world in recent years. An unprecedented development on the Western scene that has exercized a profound influence on the human sciences is what has been aptly described by Clifford Geertz as genre mixing or academic deprovincialization (Geertz, 1983: 19-35). This is reflected, for example, in the blurring of disciplinary boundaries and in the increasing employment of analogies from the humanities in the understanding and description of social reality. There is a growing feeling in academia that human and social reality is multi-layered and extremely complex and hence its texture and nuances cannot be adequately comprehended within the framework of Cartesian epistemology, which has been the reigning paradigm in the social sciences for over two centuries. There is mounting disenchantment with reductionism and fragmentation of knowledge brought about by reckless empiricism and over-specialization. The need to get back to larger and fundamental questions, such as the goal and purpose of knowledge, the bearing of social and moral responsibility on social science research and the linkage between fact and value, is being acutely felt and articulated in academic discussions. Meanings, values and symbols have come to occupy a prominent place in the discourse of the social sciences. There is evidence of greater sensitivity, on the part of Western social scientists, towards the cultural categories and intellectual traditions of non-Western peoples.

It is highly appropriate and opportune that this session of the 14th International Congress of Anthropological and Ethnological Sciences is devoted to the theme of alternative models in anthropology. In my view, the search for alternative models in the discipline should entail two major prerequisites: The identification and correction of the Eurocentric underpinnings of Western anthropology and a critical scrutiny of the relevance and utility of non-Western concepts and categories. This paper hopes to make a modest contribution in this direction by focusing on the promise and potential of the discourse of Sufism and by bringing out its contribution to the formulation of an alternative paradigm in philosophical anthropology. The paper is divided into five parts : (i) the discourse of Sufism, (ii) Sufi epistemology, (iii) the conception of human nature in Sufism, (iv) the role of the man of knowledge in the Sufi discourse and (v) towards a new vision for the science of man.

• The Discourse Of Sufism

The discourse of Sufism or Islamic mysticism is embedded in the Islamic ethos (Arberry, 1950; Schimmel, 1975; Lings, 1988). It essentially represents an interiorization of Islamic ideals and values and emphasizes the personal experience of divine majesty and mystery. Drawing inspiration from a verse of the *Quran* which says that God is closer to man than his jugular vein (50:16), the Sufi is possessed with the consciousness that every moment of his life he is in the presence of the Divine, face to face with Him, as it were. The Prophet Muhammad described this sublime experience as *ihsan* (literally, embellishment), saying that one should worship God as if he were looking at him; if this is not possible for him, he should imagine, while praying, that God is looking at him. The Sufi ethos is deeply influenced by a meta-historical event which is mentioned in the following verse of the *Quran* :

> When thy Lord drew forth from the
> Children of Adam from their loins,
> their descendants and made them
> testify concerning themselves, (saying) :
> 'Am I not your Lord?' They said :
> 'Yes, we do testify ....' (7:171).

The Sufis cherish the goal of returning to the experience of this primordial covenant between God and man. Their primary objective is the pursuit of divine love, which is attainable only through the purification of the heart. According to Junayd of Baghdad (d. 910), the doyen of Sufism, Love means giving up one's own qualities and taking on those of the beloved. Ghazali (d. 1111) says that the highest of all spiritual stations is the love of God. The Sufis look at dogmatism and ritualism with disdain. They emphasize that spiritual bliss can be attained only by qualifying oneself with the qualities of God, as mentioned in one of the sayings (*Hadith*) of the Prophet, which requires one to give up all worldly temptations and entanglements. Junayd is reported to have said : 'Sufism is not (achieved) by much praying and fasting, but it is the security of the heart and the generosity of the soul. We did not take Sufism from talk and words, but from hunger and renunciation of the world and from cutting off the things to which we were accustomed and which we found agreeable' (Qushayri, 1912 : 19).

A significant dimension of the Sufi discourse relates to hermeneutics. The Sufis maintain that the highest reaches of spiritual experience lie beyond the reach of philosophy and discursive reason; they can be communicated only through parables, anecdotes and symbols. For example, Jalaluddin Rumi (d. 1273), the celebrated Sufi poet, says 'If you plant in the earth only the kernel of an apricot, nothing will grow; if you plant it alongside its husk, then it will grow. From this we realise that the form also has a function'.

Sufi Epistemology

The views of the Sufis on knowledge and its varied dimensions are essentially derived from Islamic epistemology. It is, therefore, appropriate to present an outline of the structure of Islamic epistemology.

The Prophet Muhammad declared that the acquisition of knowledge is obligatory on all Muslims. He had a characteristically open attitude towards the pursuit of knowledge. Thus he declared : 'Wisdom is (like) the lost animal of a believer; wherever he finds it, he catches hold of it'. Unlike in other cultural, traditional and philosophical systems, the Islamic perspective on knowledge is fundamentally characterized by universalism, humanism, egalitarianism and openness (Rosenthal, 1970; Momin, 1998). Here knowledge is not the exclusive preserve or privilege of an elite or priestly class; it is open and accessible to all sections of society, regardless of the distinctions of race, caste, wealth or rank. The Prophet of Islam exhorted people to disseminate knowledge as widely as possible and warned against withholding or concealing it. Islam eschews the duality of knowledge and action; instead, it considers them in a unitary and interactional framework. The structure of Islamic epistemology is essentially normative in that the acquisition and dissemination of knowledge are informed and guided by Islamic values and ideals. Thus, knowledge is to be sought and disseminated not for its own sake or for worldly gains, but as an aid to the recognition of God and of oneself and as a guide to righteous action. A prayer of the Prophet makes a distinction between beneficial and non-beneficial knowledge. Thus the normative thrust of Islamic epistemology steers clear of the fallacies of relativism, dogmatism and scepticism. Rene Guenon has observed that the East upholds the superiority of contemplation over action, whereas the West maintains the contrary (Guenon, 1942 : 50-55). Islamic epistemology offers a corrective to such extreme views and considers contemplation and action in a unitary framework.

There is a sharp distinction between Islamic epistemology and Cartesian epistemology. The predominant conception of rationality in the Western intellectual tradition is reductionistic (Koestler, 1976; Feyerabend, 1975; Hollis and Lukes, 1982). Cartesian epistemology equates reason exclusively with scientific rationality and thereby confines the source of knowledge to sense experiences alone. Other modes of knowledge, which are as significant as the rational — empirical mode, including insight, intuition, introspection and empathy, are deemed to be unscientific and therefore unreliable. In contrast, Islamic epistemology espouses a holistic framework of knowledge, in which the rational — empirical and the extra-sensory modes of knowledge are viewed as complementary.

The principle of empiricism, which lies at the heart of Cartesian epistemology, rests on the assumption that anything which cannot be perceived through the senses or which is not measurable in quantitative or statistical terms is as good as non-existent. This methodological imperialism holds that the scientific method is applicable in equal measure to every domain of reality. A corollary of this view is that, as Roger Garoudy has observed, all problems, including those of morality, religion and politics, can be solved by the application of the scientific method (Garoudy, 1981 : 400-401). Islamic epistemology repudiates such reductionistic claims.

Another limitation of Cartesian epistemology lies in the radical separation between fact and value, between the perception of reality and its evaluation. Descartes argued that one must separate facts from values, morality and faith from the domain of reason. This dichotomy is not only illusory but also myopic. The fact of the matter is that the perception and interpretation of facts invariably entail value suppositions. Islamic epistemology stresses that one's perception and judgement should not be influenced or distorted by prejudice or other irrational factors. At the same time, it underscores the centrality of values in guiding perception and cognition.

The Sufis have made an outstanding contribution to our understanding of the dynamics of cognitive processes. They contrasted between love and discursive reason, between immediate, experientially-rooted knowledge and formal, scholastic learning. They often derided the bookishness and pedantry of scholars and theologians.

One can discern a measure of anti-intellectualism in the Sufi discourse, which is directed at idle talk, armchair theorizing and scholastic hair-splitting. Drawing inspiration from the distinction made by the Prophet between beneficial and non-beneficial forms of knowledge, the Sufis dwelt at considerable length on the 'afflictions' of knowledge. They observed that there is no necessary connection between knowledge and enlightenment and that knowledge can be a source of both guidance and misguidance.[1] They described certain forms of knowledge as a 'veil' that conceals reality. The Sufis perceptively drew a distinction between knowledge and 'talk' : they described someone endowed with deep learning and wisdom as a scholar and another with the superficial trappings of scholarship but given to pedantry and pretension as a mere 'talker'. The Sufi contribution to epistemology and cognitive anthropology is seminal and deserves to be explicated in a thoroughgoing manner (Tyler, 1969; Applebaum, 1987; Levinson and Ember, 1996).

• The Conception Of Human Nature In Sufism

One may discern, in the history of human thought, three contrasting views of human nature : (i) a benign or romantic view, according to which human nature is seen as inherently good, (ii) a cynical or negative view, which equates human nature with evil and viciousness and (iii) a neutral view, which holds that there is no such thing as original human nature and that it is largely a product of social conditioning. Socrates held that no man voluntarily pursues evil, because it is not embedded in human nature. Chinese philosophy espouses a benign view of human nature. In Europe, from the Renaissance through the Enlightenment, there developed the philosophy of humanism which regarded man as the measure of everything.

The eminent historian of ideas Arthur Lovejoy has observed that a pessimistic and cynical attitude towards man and his destiny has been the dominant strain throughout the greater part of history (Lovejoy, 1961 : 6-7). In Western Christianity, St. Augustine developed the doctrine of original sin and held that all men are born sinful. Schopenhauer (d. 1860) developed a highly pessimistic and cynical view of man. He regarded man as an evil animal who differs from other animals only in his greater viciousness. The philosophy of Neitzsche (d. 1900) contains extreme contempt and hatred for man. Reinhold Niebuhr (d. 1971) spoke of evil as being in the centre of human personality.

Under the influence of the Cartesian-Newtonian world-view, the social and human sciences sought to reduce man's nature and behaviour to mechanical and biological processes. In the 19th century, Darwinian naturalism sought to establish man's kinship with animals and viewed him as being determined by the evolutionary process. The predominant conception of man in the social and behavioural sciences is reductionistic and deterministic. The celebrated biologist Ludwig von Bertalanffy has aptly described this view as the robot model of man (Bertalanffy, 1967; Polanyi and Prosch, 1975:25). This model is still endorsed by a good many scientists. Thus, Francis Crick, who along with two colleagues won the 1962 Nobel prize for deciphering the DNA code, recently said : 'You, your joys and your sorrows, your memories and your ambitions, your sense of personal identity and free will, are in fact no more than the behaviour of a vast assembly of nerve cells' (Swerdlow, 1995:18).

The romantic as well as the cynical views of man's nature present only a partial and therefore, distorted picture of the human condition. A major limitation of romantic view of human nature is that it offers no satisfactory explanation for the universal existence of evil and viciousness in human society. The cynical and deterministic view of human nature, on the other hand, fails to take cognizance of human intervention.

There is no denying the fact that the problem of human nature is central to the science of man. It is, at the same time, the 'knottiest in its whole career' as Ernest Becker succinctly puts it (Becker, 1975:133; Geertz, 1973). Western anthropology has paid little or no attention to the conception of human nature in the non-Western traditions. Since the problem of human nature lies at the heart of anthropology, it is worthwhile to examine alternative views. An attempt is made in this section to bring out the quintessential features of the conception of human nature in the discourse of Sufism, which is essentially derived from Islamic sources.

According to the Islamic view, man is not the product of a blind process of evolution. Rather, he is said to have been created by God with a purpose. All men have descended from Adam, the primordial man and are therefore equal before Him. All humans are born innocent, untainted by original sin or guilt. Man is born with a primordial nature. The Prophet is reported to have said : 'There is not a new born who is not born in a state of nature. His parents make him a Jew, a Christian or a Magian'.

According to the Islamic view, man has been endowed with self-consciousness, reason and moral choice. He has been created in the best of moulds and given dominion over all that is in the universe. In addition, he has been honoured with being made the viceregent of God on earth. Thus he possesses infinite possibilities of being and becoming. Human nature is characterized by a certain duality or polarity. On the one hand, man has been created from clay, a lowly earthly substance (*Quran* 23:12; 32:7). On the other, God has breathed his soul into him (*Quran* 15:29). In addition, man has been given the freedom to choose between good and evil (*Quran* 76:3; 90:8-10). Thus, man possesses two kinds of potentialities : sublime and divine-like, on the one hand and base and demonic, on the other. Man tends to be impatient and greedy (*Quran* 70:19). The Prophet is reported to have said that if the son of Adam happens to possess two valleys filled with wealth, he would still crave for a third. Man has a tendency to be ungrateful, niggardly and contentious. He is prone to injustice and sometimes tends to make his own desire into an object of worship (*Quran* 45:23).

The *Quran* mentions three key dimensions of the human self : *nafs ammarah*, which drives man towards evil and viciousness, *nafs lawwamah*, which represents the conscience and which blames him for his waywardness and *nafs mutmainnah*, which connotes a state of inner peace and tranquillity. The three components point to the duality of human nature : one is a repository of benign and angelic potentialities and the other is a storehouse of evil and wickedness. The *Quran* and the Traditions of the Prophet do not rest content with a description and analysis of the human condition; they also lay down a set of ethical principles which help in the unfolding and flowering of man's benign and angel-like qualities.

The Islamic conception of human nature avoids the pitfalls of cynicism and determinism by emphasizing that man has the capacity and the freedom to overcome his organismic frailties and limitations and to actualise his inherent potentialities. It focuses on the unfolding and development of the moral person, who represents a microcosm of the Islamic vision of the larger moral universe (Al-Attas, 1985; Szasz, 1967).

Drawing on the *Quranic* view that good and evil are embedded in the structure of the human psyche, the Sufis make a distinction between the heart (*qalb*) and self (*nafs*). The heart, according to them, is the mainspring of benign and angelic qualities, including compassion, sincerity, altruism, humility and selflessness. The self, on the other hand, is the locus of base qualities and traits, such as pride, jealousy, selfishness, deceit and hypocrisy. This distinction is derived from the *Quran*, which describes the self as inciting people to evil (*Quran* 12:53), while it speaks of a 'sound heart' (*Quran* 26:89) and of a 'heart turned in devotion to God' (*Quran* 50:33). In the Sufi literature, the self has been compared to a defiant woman who tries to seduce and cheat the poor wayfarer. Sometimes, it is likened to a disobedient camel, a restive horse or mule, a black dog, a pig, a snake and the Pharaoh (Schimmel, 1975:112).

Since the self is considered the locus of evil and wickedness, the Sufis recommend a wilful and sustained defiance of its temptations and enticements. Overcoming one's organismic frailties and limitations, or 'natural qualities' as the Sufis describe it, is described as the greater *jihad* or Holy War. Qushayri (d. 1072) points out that the defiance of the desires and temptations of the self is the heart and soul of worship. Sahl al-Tustari (d. 896) says that one who has overpowered his self has gained mastery over the whole world. Abul Qasim Nasrabadi (d. 977) describes the self as a prison and deliverance from it as eternal bliss and peace.

The Sufis emphasize that though evil is programmed in the structure of the human psyche, it is amenable to critical analysis and containment. They prescribe two complementary methods for this purpose : purging one's personality of base and unworthy qualities (*takhliya* : emptying) and substituting them with sublime and virtuous qualities (*tahliya* : adornment). This methodology is inspired by a saying of the Prophet : 'Qualify yourselves with the qualities of God' (Momin, 1998b). Shihabuddin Suharwardi (d.1234) says that if someone gets into conflict with another, the latter should confront his adversary's self with his heart. Confronting someone's self with one's heart brings an end to viciousness and aggression. If one were to confront someone's self with his own self, which abounds in base qualities, there would be no end to strife and enmity. The Sufis point out that the experience of privations and suffering is one of the potent means for the domestication of the self and the purification of the heart. They prescribe a rigorous regimen of physical, moral and spiritual exercises for this purpose. Of particular importance is a set of four 'reductions': reduced food, reduced sleep, reduced talk and reduced mixing with people. Shaqiq of Balkh (d. 790) spoke of the alchemy of hunger.

As mentioned in the foregoing, the conception of human nature in the discourse of Sufism is essentially desired from the *Quran* and the sayings of the Prophet. In addition, the Sufis drew upon their own reflections and Observations. The Sufis were great travellers. Bishr al-Hafi (d. 835) used to say : 'Travel so that you may remain pure. If water remains stagnant in one place, it tends to get polluted'. The Sufis displayed remarkable sensitivity and perceptivity towards the nuances of human experience and brought them to bear on an explication of higher spiritual experiences. Thus, Shihabuddin Suharwardi draws attention to certain experiences of everyday life and points out that if a hungry man hears some good news, his hunger vanishes immediately. This also happens when one is faced with a situation of fear. In the same way, he says, a Sufi develops his latent psychic and spiritual potentialities to such a state of perfection that his body becomes subservient to his mind or soul. The satisfaction of biological needs becomes inconsequential for him. Abstaining from food for several days on end does not result in any kind of physical incapacitation or debility. Recent researches in biofeedback, neuroendocrinology and psychoneuroimmunology tend to confirm the validity of this perceptive observation.[2]

• Social Role Of The Man Of Knowledge

In most societies, men of learning appear to be a reflex of the needs and desires of their times. Furthermore, they seem to be invariably attracted to power and privilege and even willing to exchange their knowledge and talent for them. The Sophists in Athens, the Alexanderians, the theologians of the Middle Ages in Europe and the Renaissance literati hawked their learning and art and placed their services at the disposal of the powers that be. One comes across exception though, as in the case of Socrates, who gave his knowledge free and who epitomizes the role of the man of knowledge as a social critic.

In a seminal paper 'Social Role of the Man of Knowledge' Ernest Becker (1967) drew a distinction between two roles of the man of knowledge, the shamanistic and the Socratic. The shamanistic role, according to Becker, is a reflection of the status quo, of the needs and desires of a given society. The Socratic role, on the other hand, adopts a critical stance towards the values and practices of society. Becker points out that, historically, men of knowledge have followed the shamanistic model, rather than the Socratic one.

The Prophet Muhammad described scholars as heir to the legacy of the prophets. This tradition views the man of knowledge as a man of vision *and* action, as the custodian of a sacred trust and the pursuit and dissemination of knowledge as a mission or calling. Scholars are enjoined upon to function as the conscience keepers of the community. In the Islamic tradition, the man of knowledge is not an alienated individual or a disinterested and detached academic; rather, he is deeply involved in the affairs of the community and carried a social and moral commitment. The primary responsibility of the man of knowledge is to uphold the honour and dignity of his calling and to disseminate knowledge without fear or favour. Islamic history bears ample testimony to the fact that, by and large, scholars jealously guarded their intellectual independence and moral integrity. They refused, often at great personal risks and sacrifices, to place their learning at the service of vested interests or the powers that be. Islamic history is replete with instances in which eminent scholars and savants publicly rebuked the rulers for their moral lapses, tyranny and injustice and thereby displayed remarkable courage of conviction. In other words, they espoused the Socratic model of the man of knowledge.

• Towards A New Vision For The Science Of Man

Appropriately, the central theme of the 14th International Congress of Anthropological and Ethnological Sciences is 'The 21st century : The Century of Anthropology'. However, as we move towards the next century, we need to be on our guard and should not allow complacency to becloud our vision. We need to take stock of the achievements of the discipline, as well as of its shortcomings and failure. At the turn of the century, nothing short of a radical reorientation of the discipline is called for. This, in my view, entails three prerequisites. First, we should honestly confess that the quest for scientific respectability for the discipline has led to an unfortunate neglect of larger, fundamental issues, such as the goal and purpose of anthropological knowledge, the bearing of social and moral responsibility on anthropological research, the nexus between facts and values and the problem of human nature in a cross-cultural perspective. However, these questions cannot be suppressed for long. In fact, they have always nagged and tormented the sensitivity and conscience of a good many anthropologists (Gough, 1968; Redfield, 1962; Jarvie, 1964; Berreman, 1981; Momin, 1977). Anthropology needs to get back to these central questions and grapple with them in a broader cross-cultural and cross-national framework. Second, the ascendancy of Cartesian epistemology during the past two centuries has exercized a rather baneful influence on anthropology as well as on other social sciences. The fashioning of a new vision for the discipline in the 21st century requires the replacement of the outmoded Cartesian epistemology with an alternative, holistic epistemology based on a synthesis of science and ethics, of fact and value, of thought and action, of knowledge and reality (Hann, 1983). This implies the replacement of the natural science model, which has cast a heavy shadow on the development of the discipline, by an alternative model which is attuned to philosophy, art, ethics and historiography, rather than to the natural sciences. Third, much has been written on the colonial legacy and the Eurocentric underpinnings of Western anthropology. We need to undertake a critical reappraisal of the theoretical and methodological baggage of Western anthropology in the light of recent researches and developments. At the same time, the relevance and utility of conceptual categories and methodological approaches in the traditions of the non-Western world should be seriously examined. This exercise, undertaken in conjunction, will help in fashioning a new vision for the discipline.

NOTES

1. The information revolution unleashed through satellite communication and the internet has brought into sharp relief the vanity and worthlessness of certain forms of knowledge. There is considerable discussion these days about the information overload syndrome, which has affected office workers, executives, students and even scholars in the developed world. A recent survey commissioned by Reuters Business Information found that nearly 50 per cent

of 1,300 managers working in companies in UK, USA, Australia, Hong Kong and Singapore, who were interviewed, said that they suffered from information overload, as a result of which they experienced increased levels of anxiety and stress, poor performance and even headaches and chronic tiredness. More than half of them believe that the internet is making the situation worse and that information overload has adversely affected their home life and interpersonal relationship. Modern man's ability to generate information has far exceeded his ability to digest and review it. It is estimated that more information has been produced in the last thirty years than in the past five millennia.

2. The part of the brain which is the locus of emotions is chemically linked with the immune system. When a person is in a calm and happy state of mind, the brain releases natural painkillers. The immune cells are in constant communication with electromagnetic energy waves in the mind. One can, therefore, control the functioning of his immune cells by controlling his thoughts and emotions (Elkadi, 1995; Momin, 1996; Momin, 1998c).

REFERENCES

Applebaum, H. (ed.), 1987, *Perspectives in Cultural Anthropology*. New York: State University of New York Press.

Al-Attas, S.M., 1985, *Islam, Secularism and the Philosophy of the Future*. London: Mansell.

Arberry, A.J., 1950, *Sufism : An Account of the Mystics of Islam*. London: Clarendon Press.

Beattie, John, 1964, *Other Cultures*. New York: Free Press.

Becker, E., 1967, The Social Role of the Man of Knowledge (mimeographed).

——, 1969, *Angel in Armour : A Post-Freudian Perspective on the Nature of Man*. New York: George Braziller.

——, 1971, *The Lost Science of Man*. New York: George Braziller.

——, 1975, *Escape from Evil*. New York: Free Press.

Bertalanffy, Ludwig von, 1967, *Robots, Minds and Men*. New York: George Braziller

Berreman, G.D., 1981, *The Politics of Truth : Essays in Critical Anthropology*. New Delhi: South Asian Publishers.

Diamond, S.C., 1981, *In Search of the Primitive : A Critique of Civilization*. New Brunswick: Transaction Books.

Elkadi, A., 1995, *Multimodality and Immunotherapy Programme*. Panama City, Florida: Institute of Islamic Medicine for Education and Research.

Fahim, H. *et al.*, 1980, Indigenous Anthropology in non-Western Countries, *Current Anthropology*, Vol. 21, No.5, pp.644-63.

Feyerabend, Paul, 1975, *Against Method*: London : NLB.

Geertz, C., 1973, *The Interpretation of Culture*. New York : Basic Books.

——, 1983, *Local Knowledge*. New York : Basic Books.

Garoudy, R., 1989, 'The Balance Sheet of Western Philosophy in this Century', in *Towards Islamization of Disciplines*. Herndon, Virginia : International Institute of Islamic Thought.

Gough, Kathleen, 1968, 'World Revolution and the Science of Man', in *The Dissenting Academy*, T. Roszak (ed.). New York: Random House.

Guenon, R., 1942, *The Crisis of the Modern World*. London: Luzac and Co.

Hann, Norma, 1983, *Interpretive Social Science as Moral Inquiry*. New York: Columbia University Press.

Hollis, M. and S. Lukes (eds.), 1982, *Rationality and Relativism*. Oxford: Blackwell.

Jarvie, I.C., 1964, *The Revolution in Anthropology*. New York: Humanities Press.

——, 1977, 'Epistle to the Anthropologists', in *American Anthropologist*, Vol. 77, No. 2.

——, 1984, *Rationality and Relativism : In Search of a Philosophy and History of Anthropology*. London: Routledge.

Levinson, David and M. Ember (eds.), 1996, *Encyclopedia of Cultural Anthropology*. New York: Henry Holt and Co.

Leach, Edmund, 1982, *Social Anthropology*. New York: Oxford University Press.

Lings, Martin, 1988, *What is Sufism*. London.

Lovejoy, A.O., 1961, *Reflections of Human Nature*. Baltimore: The Johns Hopkins Press.

Momin, A.R., 1977, 'Comment: Standardisation and Measurement in Cultural Anthropology' (Jerry A. Modes), in *Current Anthropology*, Vol. 18, No. 2, pp.248-49.

——, 1984, 'On the Study of One's Own Culture', in *Anthropology as a Historical Science : Essays in Honour of Stephen Fuchs*, S.M. Michael and M. Bhuriya (eds.). Indore: Sat Prakashan.

——, A.R., 1996, 'Towards an Islamic Medical Anthropology', in *Journal of Islamic Medical Association of North America*, Vol. 28, No.4, pp.168-73.

——, 1998a, *The Quest for Knowledge: An Islamic Perspective*. Kuala Lumpur.

——, 1998b, *Khwaja Nizamuddin Awliya* (in Urdu). Delhi: Qazi Publishers.

——, 1998c, 'Cognitive-Behavioural Therapy in the Sufi Discourse' (forthcoming).

Nisbet, R.N., 1983, *The Sociological Tradition*. London: Heinemann.

Polanyi, M. and M. Prosch, 1975, *Meaning*. Chicago: Chicago University Press.

Qushayri, Abul Qasim, 1912, *Al-Risalah*. Cairo.

Redfield, R., 1962, *Human Nature and the Study of Society: The Papers of Robert Redfield*. Chicago: University of Chicago Press.

Rosenthal, F., 1970, *Knowledge Triumphant*. Leiden: E.J. Brill.

Schimmel, Annemarie, 1975, *Mystical Dimensions of Islam*. Chapel Hill: University of North Carolina Press.

Srinivas, M.N., 1966, *Social Change in Modern India*. Bombay: Allied Publishers.

Swerdlow, J.L., 1995, 'Quiet Miracles of the Brain', *National Geographic*, Vol. 187, No. 6, June 1995, pp.2-41.

Szasz T., 1967, 'Moral Man : A Model of Man for Humanistic Psychology', in *Challenges of Humanistic Psychology*, J.F.T. Bugental, (ed.). New York: McGraw Hill.

Tyler, S., 1969, *Cognitive Anthropology*. New York: Holt, Rinehart and Winston.

5

ANTHROPOLOGY OF SOUND

Onkar Prasad

• Introduction

By 'anthropology of sound', I mean 'a study of man's perception of sound within and around him' and by the term 'perception', 'sensory experiences which have gained meaning or significance in the life of a man' with a particular cultural orientation.

Perceptions about sound are available to a great extent in philosophical traditions of both the Oriental and the Occidental schools of thought and to a lesser extent in ethnographic studies on some primitive groups of the world.

The sound (*vak*) is conceived as *brahman* (Supreme Being) itself which formed the basis for much of later speculations about its nature and specially for the influential concept of *sabdabrahman* as formulated by the grammarian Bhartrihari: 'That imperishable *Brahman* who has no origin and no end, of which the essential nature is the word, which manifests itself into objects and from which is the creation of the Universe' (Pillai, 1971:1).

According to *Taittiriya Brahman* (28/8/4) : 'All gods, *gandharvas* (musicians), animals and men are dependent on speech. All creatures of the whole world have their existence in speech. Speech is eternal, the first descendent of the cosmic order, mother of Vedas and the navel of the world of nectar'. In the *Vedantasutra* (1.3.28), Sankara supports the evolution of the world from (causal) sound. In this text he, however, draws a mark of distinction between 'the evolution from the *brahman*' and 'evolution from the sound' from the viewpoint of causation. Whereas from the viewpoint of the former, the *brahman* is implied as the material or essential cause (*apadana karana*) and from the viewpoint of the latter, sound is implied as the only efficient cause (*nimitta karana*) (Prajnananda, 1981: 333-34). In *Sangitratnakar* (1.3.1-4) of Sarangdev, it is told that by sound the gods exist, with sound they are worshipped and the entire world process of continuous creation and dissolution subsists by means of sound (Rowell, 1992: 40).

This notion of the sound is also to be found in the Christian tradition.

God 'speaks' the word and the Thing appears. Thus the Hebrew word for Light is 'Aur'. Genesis says, 'God said: let there be Light (Aur) and there *was* Light (Aur)'. The Divine word is conceived of in the Hebrew scriptures as having creative power. A further stage of thought presents to us the concept of an aspect of the Supreme or Person who creates. Thus we have the Supreme and the Logos, *brahman* and *sabdabrahman.* In Greek, Logos means (as does *aparasabda*) thought and the word which denotes the object of thought. To Heraclitus, Logos was the principle underlying the universe. The fourth Gospel opens grandly, 'In the beginning was the Word and the Word was with God and the Word was God.' (Woodroffe, 1955:3-4).

Like the Oriental and Occidental philosophers, the Australian aborigines, as observed by Chatwin (1987), also believe that the world and its various species came into existence from the void only after the cry of their totemic ancestors. For them, sound is also definitive to the physical space, clan, kinship, marriage and all that relates to social space and the economic and ceremonial transactions.

The Maidu, a tribe of central California, while narrating their world history, refer to Wonomi who, by singing, creates the earth (Dupre, 1975:104). The Kalina, a tribe of Guyana, believe that the *aula* (word, language) of each species existed from the beginning and that it was just this *aula* that created every visible thing. They also believe that the same sound brings the structures variety into the visible world. It is the language of men and things that shows the basic unity of the world. The Kaingang share this basic concept that everything has its 'talking', the conscious experience, of a world full of 'different things' which can be expected to be counterbalanced by the meta-conscious awareness of a basic unity appearing in the responsive meaning of their hunting rituals and in the compulsive character of the words and other forms of magic (ibid. : 240).

In *Tantra Shastra*, the process of creation, *sakti* or the Supreme Energy emerges in the form of *nada* or vibration generating from *shunya* and turns into *bindu* or point as her first perceptible identity. In *sakta* terminology, the *bindu* is also styled as *ghanibhuta sakti* (energy crystallised) which stirs forth as multiple forces of the universe. The expansion of the creative process, according to *sakta* thought, produces *dhvani* (sound) or *sabda* and its numerous varieties; therefore, the Goddess is called *sabdatmika* or *sabdabrahmamayi*, *vanmayi* or *vak*, i.e. the primordial speech. The concept further evolves into the systems of *bija* (seed letter), *akshara* and *mantras* which are stated to contain within them the source of potency/power, colours and forms to be cultivated and nurtured by the initiated *sadhakas* or the devotees of *sakti* as a part of *sadhana* to achieve higher objectives. Therefore, the principle of *Dhvani* or sound whether internal or external, carries special significance in *Saktism* and it is well reflected besides the thought, in the associated rituals and symbols (Joshi, 1994:16).

The conception that the sound within itself contains the power or potency can best be made explicit by understanding the structure and significance of the term *mantra*. 'A *mantra* is composed of letters. Letters and their combinations as syllables and words are all forms of manifested *sabda*, that is *brahman*-forms. They are each and all forms of the creative stress, as uttered by the mouth, heard by the ear and apprehended by the mind; but what are ordinarily called *mantras* are those particular sounds which are used in worship and practice (*sadhana*) which consist of certain letters, or letters arranged in a definite sequence of sounds of which the letters are the representative signs. The relations of *varna*, *nada*, *bindu*, vowel and consonant in a *mantra* constitute the *devata* in varying forms. Certain *vibhutis* or aspects of the *devata* are inherent in certain *varnas*. The *mantra* of a *devata* is that letter or combination of letters which reveals the *devata* to the consciousness of the *sadhaka*, who has evoked it by *sadhanasakti*. The form of a particular *devata* therefore appears out of the particular *mantra* of which that *devata* is the *adhisthatri-devata*. This *mantra* is intoned in the proper way according to letter (*varna*) and rhythm (*svara*). For these reasons a *mantra*, when translated ceases to be *mantra*, that is, the sound heard and uttered in the translation are not the body of and do not evoke, the *devata*. We are then not dealing with the same sound but with a translation in another language, with other sounds giving the meaning to the intellect of the Sanskrit *mantra*. This shows that *mantra* is not mere individual thinking but a particular sound-body of consciousness. 'A *mantra* again is not the same thing as prayer or self-dedication (*atma-nivedana*). Prayer is conveyed in what words the worshipper chooses and bears its meaning on its face. It is only ignorance of *shastrik* principles which supposes that *mantra* is merely the name for the words in which one expresses what one has to say to the divinity. If it were, the *sadhaka* might choose his own language without recourse to the external and determined sounds of *shastra*' (Woodroffe, 1955:258-60).

Besides *tantrik* philosophers, anthropologists have expounded the ethnographic theory of magical power of a word. Malinowski for example (*The Coral Gardens and their Magic*, Vol. 2) reports that the Trobrianders make a distinction between the language of magic (*megwa la biga*) and the language of ordinary speech (*livala la biga*). He outlines some features of the language of magic:

(1) It is sacred and is set apart from ordinary linguistic uses. It contains distinct prosodic features including even 'meaningless' words which are supposed to exercise special influence;
(2) It has the basis of native belief in a world pervaded by sympathetic affinities and powerful forces but more importantly the belief that it is man-made, existed from the very beginning as primeval text coeval with reality and could be launched as 'breath' and transformed into magical missiles by accredited magicians; and
(3) It contains the 'coefficient of weirdness' and this was indexed by strange and archaic grammatical forms, condensed structures, words containing esoteric meanings and strange mythological and metaphorical references and allusions (as he said, weirdness yields to treatment as soon as we place the spells within their context) (c.f. Tambiah, 1993 : 74).

• HYPOTHESES

On the basis of the above perceptions of sound in different philosophical and cultural traditions, the following workable propositions may be formulated :

(a) That sound inheres the basic principle of differentiation as well as unification of all things of the universe;
(b) That sound is causal to the cosmological process of creation, dissolution and recreation; and
(c) That sound which contains the power or potency is efficacious.

This aims at examining these assumptions in the sociocultural context of the Santhal, one of the largest tribal communities settled throughout Eastern India, who are racially proto-Australoid and linguistically part of the Munda group of Austro-Asiatic sub-family.

The Santhal, like many other tribal groups of India, operate within the agrarian economic structure of the caste society, but at the same time live in a world of dynamic isolation perpetuating a distinct social and cultural life.

This paper examines the Santhal perception of sounds of different origins — humans, animals and birds, air, ether, water, fire, earth, plants and other material objects that constitute their acoustic environment and influence their cognition and connotation in day-to-day life. For this three Santhal villages (Baradanga Sarpalehana, Bandlodanga and Koetpukur around Sriniketan, West Bengal) were selected.

• Ethnographic Data And Their Analysis

Among the Santhal, the common term for sound is *sade*. Various types of sounds produced by different objects that constitute their soundscape, are classified mainly under three categories - *sade*, *aran* and *rak*.

The term *sade* is used to refer to sounds produced by different objects as a result of a stroke or collision or friction. Sounds included under this category are those of men, animals and insects, other than their calls and those of material objects, e.g., *hoe sade* (whizzing of the air), *dak' sade* (sound of water), *rimil sade* (roaring of the cloud), *tamak sade* (sound of the kettledrum), etc.

The term *aran* is used to refer to the purely human voice, e.g., *tala nindere hor aran anjomkate setako rak keda* (Having heard the voice of man, the dog started barking). The rhythmic as well as tonal sounds produced by different musical instruments are also referred to as *aran*, e.g. *tumdak bhagi ban aranok kana* (The *tumdak* is not sounding well).

The term *aran* is further divided into two sub-categories — *ror* (speech sound) e.g., *horko roreda* (men are speaking) and *rar* (melodic sound), e.g. *baha rar* (*baha* melody), *sohrae rar* (*sohrae* melody) etc. But according to the Santhals there is no sharp distinction between the two, i.e., *ror* and *rar*. There is famous aphorism among them - *roraktege rarak* (melody is the prolongation of the ordinary speech).

The term *rak* is used to refer to the sounds produced by different animals and birds and insects, e.g. *setako rakkeda* (the dogs are barking), *cercetece rakkeda* (the house lizard is calling), *sime rakkeda* (the cock is calling), etc.

The sound produced by a man experiencing pain is also termed as *rak*, e.g. *kirir kirir* (sound of crying loudly) and *kusuk kusuk* (sound of sobbing), etc.

Though the Santhals apparently make a distinction between *jiwet* (living) and *goc* (dead) elements of nature and other living beings (i.e., animals, birds and insects), yet this becomes non-existent in the case of rhythmic sounds (i.e. when an inanimate object is moved or is in use). For example, the term *aran* is used to refer to both the sounds produced by man and that by musical instrument when being played. Again, the distinction between man and other living beings specially birds, becomes non-existent. The painful cry of human beings and the call of the birds are both referred to as *rak*. What emerges from this observation is the following : that the various categories of sounds among the Santhal are not exclusive but interconnected. That in Santhal thought, sound inheres the basic principle of differentiation as well as unification of all things of their universe — spatial and temporal.

Among the Santhal, there are two percussions - the *tamak*, a bowl shaped kettle-drum and the *tumdak*, a cylindrical drum - which are always played in accompaniment with music and dance associated with annual and life cycle rituals. The *ru* term stands for the beat produced on them such as the *sohrae ru, baha ru* and *don ru*. The beating of these drums especially with dance is accomplished in four steps: *ru-ehop* (opening drumbeat), *ru-calti* or *sardi* (continuing drumbeat), *ru-toraw* (changing drumbeat) and *ru-mucet* (the final drumbeat). The opening drumbeat indicates the beat-pattern which accompanies the dance to follow. It creates the necessary mood and keeps the dancer in readiness. It is a complete form in itself and lasts for a short duration. The continuing drumbeat is a dance drumbeat. It is the beat of the longest duration. The changing drumbeat usually alters the form, by bringing changes into the style of drumming. The final drumbeat is brought to an end either by shifting from the changing drumbeat to the opening drumbeat or with a different set of rhythmic phrases (Hembram 1976 : 29). This is illustrated (Appendix - I) with the help of some *baha* drumbeats collected from Baradanga during the *baha* (flower) festival celebrated during spring-time when the first shoots on the trees appear symbolizing manifestation or re-manifestation of life on the earth.

The Santhals beat their drums generally in four steps viz '*ru-ehopi, ru-sardi, ru-toraw* and *ru-mucet*' respectively. In the first step they create a form, in the second they evolve or elaborate it, in the third they break or destroy the earlier form to create a new form and finally in the fourth step they come to an end generally by repeating the form created in the beginning. This observation suggests that in Santhal thought sound is subservient to the basal principle of cosmology viz. creation,[1] dissolution and recreation. However, this does not nullify the assumption that sound is causal to the cosmological process of creation, dissolution and re-creation but indirectly supports it as it is through the former that the latter is revealed.

Further there are some forms of human sounds which the Santhals consider powerful and hence efficacious. One such form is the *mantar*, which is composed of syllables and their combinations as words and it is classified in term of the purpose it serves. As recorded in the field situation, the *mantar* is used for *tol*, i.e. to insulate : (a) the *akhra* (a temporarily consecrated space), (b) the *ato* (village), (c) the *dahar* (street), (d) the *disam* or *dharti* (country or earth), (e) the *hormo* (body) and (f) the *orak* (house) for protection from the disturbance created by a witch, the evil eyes, the evil spirits, epidemic, catastrophe, etc. In addition to these, the *mantar* is used to seal a *gidra* (child) by the witch to create trouble in its delivery; a *jivi* (life) by the sorcerer to save the life of a dying person; and the *batik* (air) to stop the poison spreading over the body of a snake-bitten person. Here is an example of the *mantar* which is used to insulate the *akhra* when the disciples have finished their evening lesson by the *ojha* guru, the combatives like the '*pak don, ghawa eneć*', etc. are taught by its specialist; and the dance is held outside the village on a fixed place specially on the occasion of the *corok*, the 'hook-swinging' festival of the Santhals. The text of the *mantar* means as follows :

I sealed the *akhra* at the time of leaving it, I sealed the *pir* at the time of leaving it, I sealed the temple at the time of leaving it. Then who seals? The Guru seals. By the order of Guru I seal. It is sealed. By the grace of the country of *Siri Kari Karu*.

The *mantar* is also used for *rara*, i.e., for opening (a) the *akhra*, when leaving it or when entering it and (b) the *hormo* for releasing a witch when her body has been sealed by means of the *mantar*. Subsequently the *mantar* is used for *sompa*, i.e., for entrusting some malignant spirits to do harm to the people of a house or a village or an area. Here is an example of the *mantar* which is used for 'opening' the *akhra* when the disciples learning the *Ojha* science come to take the evening lesson from the second day onwards as on the first day and the Santhal boys learn *baji* (acrobatics) under the supervision of a trained teacher. The *mantar* runs as follows : 'The training starts after the *akhra* is opened, who opens? The Guru opens. By the order of the Guru the mother opens. It is opened by the order of *kahri*, by the order of the mother, by the order of *kahri* of *kamrup*, by the grace of the mother'.

The *mantar* is further used for *pachao*, i.e. for divining or diagnosing the various causes of sickness or afflictions by the natural or unnatural.

Lastly, the *mantar* is used for *katan*, i.e., for the treatment of the patient believed to be under the influence of any malignant spirit.

These observations prove the assumption that sound which contains the power or potency is efficacious.

APPENDIX - I

Ehop

1	2	3	1	2	3	1	2	3	1	2	3
Da	ti	-n	da	ti	-n	da	ta	-n	ti	-	-n'
Dak'	-	-ta	he	ta	-n	da	ta	-n	ti	-	-n'
Dak'	.	.	da	ta	-n	da	ta	-n	ti	-	-n'
Da	-	-n									

Sardi

Jan	dob	ti	-n'	jan	dob	da	-n	
Jan	dob	ti	-n'	jan	dob	da	ran	
Jan	dob	ti	-n'	jan	dob	da	-n	
Jan	dob	ti	-n'	jan	dob	dak'	tan	
ti	-n'							
ti	-n'	jan	dob	da	-n	jan	dob	(3)
ti	-n'	jan	dob	da	-n	jan	dob	(10)

Toraw

1	2	3	1	2	3	1	2	3	1	2	3
Dak'	tan		dak'	-		ti	-n		jan	dob	
da	n										
Dak'	-	da	tin'	dak'		da	ti	-n	ja	pu-t'	
						Da	ta	-n	da	ti	-n

Sardi

da	ti	-n'	ja	pu	-t'						
						Phe	-	-t'	Phe	ti	-n'
da	ta	-n'	ti	-	-n'						
						da	ti	-n'	da	ti	-n'
da	ta	-n	da	ti	-n'	jan	do	-b	ti	-	-n
Da	ta	-n	da	ti	-r	da	ti	-n	ti	-	-n'
Da	ta	-n	da	ti	-r	jan	do	-b	ti	-	-n'
He	ta	-n	da	nda	-n	da	ta	-n	ti	-	-n'
Da	ta	-n	da	ti	-n'	jan	do	-b	da	-	-n

MECET'

Da	ta	-n	da	ti	-r	jan	do	-b	da	ra	-n
Da	-	-n									
Dak'	-	-	da	ti	-r	jan	do	-b	da	ra	-n
Da	-	n									

NOTE

1. There is a story among the Santhals suggesting that the sound is causal to the creation of a thing of the universe. The story goes, 'In the beginning, *Maran Buru*, the Great Mountain, instructed *Pilcu Haram Na Pulcu Budhi*, the primeval couple of the Santhal tribe, to go to a forest to bring *ran* (the root of a plant) to be added in the preparation of rice-beer. There, following the instruction of *Maran Buru*, they uttered *ranuran*. Then, there appeared the tree. The couple went close to the tree and said that they would like to take away its *ran* to prepare the rice-beer. The tree said 'You can, but it may intoxicate you, make you laugh, quarrel and sing songs'. Both, however, without caring about the warning the tree gave to them, took away the root, prepared the rice-beer and drank it which caused *Pilcu Haram* and *Pulcu Budhi* to indulge in sex-acts. This pleased *Maran Buru*. Later seven sons and eight daughters were born to them'.

REFERENCES

Chatwin, Bruce, 1987, *The Songlines*. London: Pan Books Ltd.

Dupre, Wilhelm, 1975, *Religion in Primitive Cultures: A Study in Ethnophilosophy*. The Mouton.

Hembram, P.C., 1976, 'The Drumbeat in Santhal Culture', in *Journal of the Sangeet Natak Akademi*. 39.

Joshi, M.C., 1994, 'Conceptual Aspects of Sound in *Saktism*', in *Nature and Culture of Sound*, S.C. Malik (ed.). New Delhi: IGNCA and D.K. Printworld.

Pillai, K.R., 1971, *The Vakyapadiya : Critical Text of Cantos I & II*. Delhi: Motilal Banarasidass.

Prasad, Dineshwar, 1989, *Loksahitya Aur Sanskriti*. Allahabad: Jayabhartiya Prakashan.

Prajnananda, Swami, 1981, *A Historical Study of Indian Music*. Delhi: Munshiram Manohorlal Publishers Pvt. Ltd.

Rowell, Lewis, 1992, *Music and Musical Thought in Early India*. Chicago: University of Chicago Press.

Tambiah, S.J., 1993, *Magic, Science, Religion and the Scope of Rationality*. Cambridge: Cambridge University Press.

Woodroffe, S.J., 1955, *The Garland of Letters (Varnamala) : Studies in the Mantra-Shastra*. Madras: Ganesh & Co. (Madras) Ltd.

PART II

SPACE AND TIME

6

CULTURAL CONCEPTS OF SPACE AND TIME

Molly Kaushal

• Introduction

Anthropologists of religion view the order of things, real or ideal, into two classes, two models of being in the world. Terms such as pure/impure, sacred/secular, transcendental/physical, auspicious/inauspicious are used to grasp the realities of practical functioning and organizational principles of various social groups. At times, these categories are seen as distinct and oppositional in character and at others, as ambiguous, ambivalent and often with overlapping boundaries.[1]

My study of concepts of space and time among the Gaddis of Bharmour in Western Himalayas suggests that 'sacred' and 'secular' are not necessarily always seen as separate domains representing two sets of realities, one ideological and conceptual, other empirical and practical. Space is held to be sacred in substance and no part of it is defiled or defiling. This space is not an amorphous mass, an unbounded entity, or an abstract void.[2] It is as much a temporal space as a transcendental one, representing the infinite and eternal. It possesses the benign as well as the malignant aspects. Human activity, when in accordance with the prescribed code of conduct (*dharma*), ensures 'well-being'. Transgression of code brings calamity.[3] Calamity, arising as a consequence, is also seen as a self-cleansing/purifying act of the divine substance, inherent in space. The 'divine' has the capacity to withstand the 'contaminating act' for some time, beyond which it retaliates and purges the 'impure'. The concept of 'purity' is understood at two levels: 'clean' (free from dirt) and 'pure' (undefiled). The space is inherently 'pure'. An immoral action can make the place 'unclean'. 'Purity' is maintained by a self-regulating, self-revealing and self-restoring procedure, which is understood as an attribute of the divine. The 'non-contaminated' state, called *nirmal*, is a prerequisite for the well-being of the society. One of my informants Nanku put it this way:

If the wind is non-contaminated, the water will be non-contaminated. If the water is non-contaminated, the earth will be non-contaminated. If the earth is non-contaminated, it will bring forth non-contaminated produce. If the food is non-contaminated, it will make the mind non-contaminated. If the mind is non-contaminated, it will make the body non-contaminated. If the body is non-contaminated, it makes the society non-contaminated. This non-contaminated state can exist, only when each of these, along with cosmic beings/phenomena, maintain their rhythm by being dutiful.

It is held that each existing person has been assigned a specific rhythm and role. The rhythm (flow) of the universe depends upon maintaining the individual rhythm through right performance. This notion of a continuous rhythm and the cardinal principle of gender are the points of reference through which the Gaddi categories of space and time are expressed, understood and conceptualized.

- Space

Categories of space and time are conceptually derived from an upward-downward movement of the Gaddi's main deity, lord Shiva, who like the Gaddis, is a nomad and a shepherd. He is believed to spend one-half of the year on the Mount *Mani Mahesh*, 36 km east of Bharmour and the other half in nether-land. The migratory pattern of the Gaddis coincides with the migratory pattern of their principal deity. Their annual calendar of activities is divided into two halves, representing two distinct modes of life. In summer they move up to Bharmour and the high passes of Dholadhar; in winter they move down to the low valley of Kangra.

The Gaddi space is formed around a vertical axis. On the one end of the axis is Shiva's *Kailash*, on the other end is nether-land. The upward-downward movement on this axis is cyclical and it follows the natural rhythm. When Shiva migrates to nether- land, he takes away with him all the living creatures. The Gaddis also migrate along with him. Before migrating they make a pilgrimage to Mount *Mani Mahesh Kailash*. This pilgrimage in many ways recreates and replicates the first ever visit by a human being to the holy abode of Shiva. It also reflects the Gaddi seasonal migratory pattern. This upward-downward movement along the vertical axis is so important, that it is reflected in their more sedentary existence as well, namely, in the settlement pattern, construction of houses and life within the house, which also follows this seasonal upward-downward movement. The Gaddi language also reflects this emphasis on verticality by situating objects mostly on an upward-downward movement.

The notion of verticality is present also in the way the Gaddi conceives the creation of the world from a primeval tree. The tree is divided vertically into three parts, creating three worlds along with their inhabitants. This primal image of the emerging world gets translated into a symbolic representation of the Gaddi land, where the original image of the *arbour mundi* embedded in primeval waters, appears in the form of an *axis mundi* (*Mani Mahesh*) and the water reservoir (*yoni*-basin).

To a Gaddi this space is both immediate and physical on the one hand and metaphysical and transcendental on the other. The area where the Gaddi lives and tends his flock is the majestic Dholadhar range. This pasture land rests in Parvati's lap, the *yoni*-basin of Shiva. The space here is conceptualized in terms of Shiva-Parvati continuum. The Gaddi sees himself as an extension of this space. The Gaddi body, created with a speck of dust from Shiva's body; the Gaddi garb, a symbolic extension of Shiva's own self; the Gaddi cap, whose top represents Shiva's *Kailash* and the flaps of the cap that represent the inner chambers of Parvati's abode repeat the same continuum. The Shiva *bhumi* (holy land of Shiva), that protects and nurtures the Gaddi has the central axis of its existence in lord Shiva, who himself is embedded in this land as Mount *Mani Mahesh*. Horizontally viewed *Mani Mahesh* stands in the Centre of the earth. On the either side of it stretches the human world. Earth is the homeland of humans, animals, deities, spirits and demons all at once. Viewed vertically, *Mani Mahesh* stands at the topmost axis, from where there can be no journey beyond.

- TIME

Life on this earth has a rhythm. Time defines and is defined by a prescribed code of conduct, *dharma*. Both cosmic and cultural structures are maintained by *dharma*. Gradual deviation in *dharma* follows the cycle of *yuga*. When order collapses totally, the cosmic rhythm is broken and dissolution follows.

Gaddi divisions of annual calendar and seasonal cycles are both empirical and conceptual. At the conceptual level the physical time is computed metaphorically in terms of germination and growth. The year is divided into four seasons: winter, spring, rains and autumn. The seasonal cycle is categorized into two spells: (a) spring and rainy seasons, conceived as an 'immature' and 'unripe' spell; and (b) autumn and winter, a 'matured' and a 'fully ripe' spell. 'Immature season' is wet. It symbolises the beginning of new life. During this period the seed germinates, sprouts and flowers. Towards the end of this spell it begins to ripen. Autumn is the beginning of 'mature season', when crops mature. Harvesting begins only after the gods and ancestors have properly been propitiated for one full month. Agricultural cycle starts in April, with the sowing of maize and ends in October with the sowing of wheat. The winter, though perceived as a healthy and mature season, is considered to be dry and non-fertile. Spring and rainy seasons, though fertile, are regarded as unhealthy, because of the presence of excess water (*rasa*), which is regarded as a feminine entity. Its spatial counterpart is the image of Shiva's water reservoir (*jalhairi*). Excess of water *(rasa)* weakens the blood (which is a masculine entity) and causes loss of vigour. This wet spell is thought to be hot from outside and cold from inside (the reason why it is unhealthy). The water attracts the seed and holds it inside, providing it with the ground to germinate. Sixteen days of incessant rains, followed by 16 days of scorching sunshine, known as fecundating sun-rays in the month of August, are crucial for germination, sprouting and ripening of the seed. In fact, the sunshine helps the sprouted seed to reach its matured state by decreasing the water. Water gradually turns into fat. The blood increases and dry spell sets in. This spell is cold from outside but hot from inside. Devoid of water, it is sterile. Nothing germinates in this season. The seed lies underneath the ground waiting for the wet spell to begin so that it may sprout.

The biological principle follows the cosmological principle realised in Shiva, the primal seed. Identification of Shiva with the primal seed is stated clearly in the Gaddi religious epic *Saveen*. Every Gaddi, at least once in his life time, performs a special Shiva worship — *Nuala*, to repay his debt to this primal seed. The performance of *Nuala* geometrically reconstructs the Gaddi vision of the universe and symbolically celebrates the primeval act of creation. Rituals, conducted during the ceremony along with the performance of Gaddi oral epic, are a collective recalling of community's memory of its history, land and people on the one hand and of the universe and its lord on the other. In this consecrated space and circumscribed time, at the ceremony of *Nuala*, the Gaddis symbolically overcome the boundaries of the 'local' and 'universal', of the 'history' and 'cosmology', of the 'terrestrial' and 'cosmic,' of the 'self' and 'other' and of the 'space' and 'time'.[4]

• Space, Time, Number

During *Nuala*-worship, a 32-square *Mandala* of the four cornered earth is drawn with wheat flour on the ground. On its four corners are drawn four mounts, representing 4 *Kailashas*. In the centre of the *Mandala* stands Mount *Sumeru*. Shiva is invited to dwell on the top of the mount. A garland made of nine woollen strings is hung over the central mount. These strings symbolize nine streams of the celestial *Ganga*. The entire *Mandala* brings to the mind the *Vastu-Purusha Mandala* (the Indian temple design) of 64 squares. This 32-square *Mandala* represents the micro model of the macrocosm, which is represented by the cardinal number 84. Among the Gaddis, 32 and 84 are important spatial numbers.

The feminine principle, representing the horizontal space in the Gaddi mythology, is expressed through the images of womb, pot and water reservoir, which contain the fecund feminine waters. Numerically, this place is represented through the number 32. Earth is represented by 8 × 4 *Mandala*. It is believed that the female body has 32 doors leading to the womb. The womb itself consists of eight doors and four sides. The mother's milk is said to consist of 32 streams, 16 in each breast. Parvati, Shiva's consort, is represented by a 16-square *Mandala*. Though predominantly a spatial number, it also signifies the temporal dimension of physical growth. The seed grows inside the female waters and feeds on 32 streams of milk. These last in a man till the age of 32. After this the growth stops. The decline in vigour starts thereby indicating the completion of the physical growth. This is the end of a young immature state closely bound with its female beginnings. The notion of 'immature' season, discussed above, expresses the same idea in another context. Separation from the female beginnings indicates maturity on the one hand and a period of non-growth, gradual decay and a non-fertile, purely male state on the other.[5]

The notion of verticality is represented by the number three. The world is divided into three parts. The world as a whole is sevenfold; hence, vertical in this context is three times seven. The vertical body, the micro-model of the universe has three parts. The primeval body of the universe is visualized as threefold: the head, from where Shiva was conceived; the chest, from where Brahma was conceived; and feet, from where Vishnu was conceived. The Gaddi house, which stands, as if on a vertical pole, has three storeys and is a micro model of the universe. Growth of the seed into harvest has three stages of development. The *arbour mundi* is divided into three parts. Earth consists of three layers: the outermost consists of vertical *Kailash* and horizontal *jalhairi*; the second layer is vertical Bull (*Dhola Bail*) and horizontal slate (*Bajar Sila*); the last layer contains vertical snake *Vasuki* and horizontal lotus flower. All these layers floating in the primeval waters are located in Shiva's eye, 84 Mahadev.

The number 84 includes both the vertical and the horizontal dimensions of space, as well as the third dimension of time. Shiva is believed to have

84 forms (84 *Mahadev*), his *jamat* consists of 84 *Siddhas*. The initial number of sheep, which Shiva gave to the Gaddi is 84. The Gaddi promises to sacrifice 84 sheep to Shiva on the occasion of his wish-fulfilment. The Gaddi epic refers to 84 mountain ranges of the world. It also talks of 8.4 million deities in the sky. The Gaddi cosmic calendar consists of 12 months, 24 fortnights, 27 asterisms, nine planets and 12 zodiac signs. The journey of the sun and moon through these completes a year, both solar and lunar. Possibly the original symbolism of 84 was derived from this annual cycle of the sun and moon through the astral bodies, the sum total of which yields the number 84.

The number 84 represents not only the year, but also the completion of the great cycle of 84 forms of existence of the soul (84 *joon*). Each soul is supposed to go through 8.4 million subtle or gross forms of existence before it completes one full circle of births and deaths (*Kala Chakra*), after which the cycle starts afresh. The number 84 thus, stands for both the vertical and horizontal spaces according to $3 \times 7 \times 4$ model. It also denotes the completion of a temporal cycle of time: both the solar and the lunar year and the great circle of births and deaths.

The number 84 figures in yet another prominent way. An important temple complex in Bharmour is called *Chaurasi* (i.e., 84). It contains 84 *shivalingas* representing 84 *siddhas*. It is held as the original celestial kingdom (not a reflection or a replica, but the real kingdom). Believed to be situated in the *yoni*-basin (*jalhairi*) of Shiva, it remains intact during the cosmic dissolution. This temple complex, which in its design and mythology resembles a cosmogram, encapsulates the Gaddi vision of complete space and absolute time.

• Conclusion

The Gaddi vision of space is one of eternal union of Shiva and Parvati, forming the masculine-feminine continuum. The space thus envisioned is inherently pure, non-contaminated and auspicious.[6] The number 84, which encapsulates this vision is the most complete and auspicious number. It expresses the boundedness of the universe in an eternal embrace of ever flowing cosmic rhythm.

Time, like space, is also conceptualized in terms of Shiva-Parvati continuum. The metaphors of the seed and the womb are temporal symbols of Shiva and Parvati in the same manner as the spatial symbols of the *arbour mundi* and the pot, or the Mount *Mani Mahesh* and the *yoni*-basin.

Shiva is identified with the seed; seed with time. Seed represents vertical growth. Parvati represents change. She disappears at the time of cosmic dissolution and is created anew at the beginning of each new cycle of time. She, as a womb (*yoni*), indicates the new physical form (both biological and social) of the soul, which moves from one birth to another. The cycle of birth and death is often thought of as change from one womb to another.

Shiva as 84 Mahadeva, holds all that constitutes the universe in his eye, embodies and goes beyond Space and Time, Masculine and Feminine. The Gaddi religious oral narrative about Shiva's life represents a chronological account of events. It talks about the biological and social rhythm of Shiva the king, Shiva the hunter, Shiva the groom and Shiva the householder. This rhythm expands and merges into the cosmic rhythm of Shiva, the lord of the universe.

The individual, or the biological rhythm is linear in which man takes birth, grows and dies. This linear passing of time among the Gaddis is marked by tying a knot on a rope at the time of birth and subsequently on each birthday till death. At death this rope is not burnt but immersed in waters. The individual rhythm, which is linear, measurable and socially punctuated dimension of life, now merges with the ceaseless cyclical flow of the universal rhythm[7].

Shiva, the transcendental one, prepares a new spatial enclosure (gross body) for the soul, endows it with an individual rhythm and sends it back into the physical, linear space – time continuum. Here the individual aligns his own rhythm with the social and cosmological rhythms of his society and by doing so, contributes to his own, his group's and this universe's auspicious existence.

NOTES

1. For a detailed discussion of these categories see works by Das (1977, 1982), Dumont (1970), Khare (1976), Madan (1980), Marglin (1977, 1983, 1985), Saraswati (1991, 1996), Srinivas (1952), Vatsyayan (1991, 1996).
2. Kramrisch (1991) while exploring the concept of the 'space' in a wider Hindu context writes that space is the first and foremost phenomenon of creation in Indian cosmogony. This space is bounded by the firm structure of heaven and earth. Space here is not perceived as a void. It 'is a substance, a subtle, quintessential substance perceptible sensorially...', pp. 101-02.
3. Saraswati (1991) in an exposition on the nature of sacred space in a tribal–non-tribal context observes that the Sanatanis hold the whole earth to be sacred. He classifies the sacred space into (a) 'purity space' and (b) 'protection space'. *'However the effectiveness of the sacred space lasts only so long as it remains*

free from physical or moral pollution'. And this can be achieved, as seen also in case of the Gaddis, only by adhering to a prescribed code of conduct (emphasis mine), p. 857.

4. In the context of ritual performance, Vatsyayan (1991) writes, 'The consecration of space in circumscribed time is the strategy for communion of the physical and metaphysical, human and mythical, specific and universal, micro and macro', p. 394.

5. Not surprisingly then, the Gaddi groom, before departing for bride's house rejuvenates his power to procreate by sucking on his mother's breasts. In other words, he revives the fecund female energies in him. The main marriage ceremony among the Gaddis is *lagan*, which consists of a simple but a very symbolic act. The father of the bride places a fried wheat cake ('*babru*', which signifies the male seed) in the hands of the bride and the groom held one above the other and supported from below by his own hand. The mother of the bride sprinkles water from above over the *babru*. This brings to the mind the *Prithavi mandala*, drawn during the ceremony of *Nuala*, where *Sumeru Parvat Kailash* embedded in the *Prithavi Kund* is drenched by nine streams of celestial Ganga from above.

The construction of the *Prithavi mandala* in a way symbolizes the construction of a house/womb for Shiva, the primal seed to germinate. For *Prithavi* disappears during the cosmic dissolution, only the lone seed remains. Shiva after vanquishing various demons, who had been disturbing peace on earth, goes seeking for *Gorja* and asks her to provide him with *sparkling* waters:

> 'On your way there were several ponds. What kind of waters do you seek?' Gorja asks teasingly. 'All the ponds are filled with the blood of slain demons. I seek the non-contaminated water (*kanchan jal*)', Shiva replies. He eventually wins her in marriage.

6. Marglin (1985) in the context of *devdasis* of Puri concludes: '... the union of the male and the female, be it sexual one, or an androgynous one, signifies the static state of auspiciousness', p. 299.

7. Saraswati (1996), while discussing the Maithil-Indian space-time continuum, dwells on the nature of the universe, which is perceived as a continuum of dynamism between Heaven and Earth. This tradition comes very close to the Gaddi perception of space and time. He writes, 'Life and death are not in opposition. On the contrary, they are the rhythms of biological time, *Biological time is the rhythm of cosmic time and cosmic time is the rhythm of infinite rhythms of transcendental time. Change is cyclical. But within the cyclical order there is a linear progress; and then the layers of progress and decay... Creation (Srishsti), existence (sthiti) and dissolution (pralya) are the inexorable laws of natural time*'... (p. 249). Dwelling on the nature of Great Time, he expounds:

'Great Time is fundamental. It creates all forms and destroys them all, but itself remains formless. It transcends everything, but nothing transcends it. It is both linear and cyclical, measurable and immeasurable, with and without quality. *What constitutes man and the cosmos is the rhythm of time*' (emphasis mine) p. 249.

REFERENCE

Das, Veena, 1977, *Structure and Cognition: Aspects of Hindu Caste and Ritual.* Delhi: Oxford University Press.

——, 1982, Epilogue, in *Structure and Cognition,* 2nd ed. Delhi: Oxford University Press.

Dumont, Louis, 1970, (1966), *Homo Hierarchicus: The Caste System and its Implications (trans. Mark Sainsbury).* Chicago: University of Chicago Press.

Khare, R.S. 1976, The *Hindu Hearth and Home.* New Delhi: Vikas Publishing House Pvt. Ltd.

Kramrisch, Stella, 1991. Space in Indian Cosmogony and in Architecture', in *Concepts of Space: Ancient and Modern,* Kapila Vatsyayan, (ed.), pp. 101-104. New Delhi: IGNCA and Abhinav Publications.

Madan, T.N. 1985, 'Concerning the Categories *subha* and *suddha* in Hindu Culture : An Exploratory Essay', in *Purity and Auspiciousness in Indian Society,* J.B. Carman and F.A. Marglin, (eds.), pp. 11-29. *Journal of Developing Societies,* Vol. 1, fasc. 1 June (Leiden: E.J. Brill).

Marglin, Frederique, 1977, 'Power, Purity and Pollution: Aspects of the Caste System Reconsidered', in *Contributions to Indian Sociology* (n.s.), 11, 2.

——, 1983, 'Types of Oppositions in Hindu Culture', in *Purity and Auspiciousness in Indian Society.* J.B. Carman and F.A. Marglin (eds.), pp.65-83. *Journal of Developing Societies,* Vol. 1, fasc: 1 (Leiden: E.J. Brill).

——, 1985, *Wives of the God-King: The Rituals of the Devadasis of Puri.* Delhi: Oxford University Press.

Saraswati, B.N., 1991, 'Ritual Space : Tribal–Nontribal Context', in *Concepts of Space: Ancient and Modern,* Kapila Vatsyayan (ed.), pp. 355-62. New Delhi: IGNCA and Abhinav Publications.

——, 1996, 'Ritual Time: An Exegesis of Time and Great Time', in *Concepts of Time: Ancient and Modern,* Kapila Vatsyayan, (ed.), pp.248-65. New Delhi: IGNCA and Sterling Publishers Pvt. Ltd.

Srinivas, M.N., 1978, *Religion and Society Among the Coorgs of South India.* Bombay: Asia Publishing House.

Vatsyayan, Kapila, 1991, 'Performance: The Process, Manifestation and Experience, in *Concepts of Space: Ancient and Modern,* Kapila Vatsyayan, (ed.), pp.381-94. New Delhi: IGNCA and Abhinav Publications.

——, (ed.), 1996, *Concepts of Time: Ancient and Modern.* New Delhi: IGNCA and Sterling Publishers Pvt. Ltd.

7

UNIVERSALITIES AND SPECIFICITIES IN THE AFRICAN CONCEPTION OF SPACE AND TIME

Osaga Odak

• INTRODUCTION

The way space and time are conceived is related to and reflects the culture of the conceivers. Such a conception mirrors the cultural system itself and determines the relationship between it and its bearers. However, there is no clear evidence for the existing relationship between the way people within a culture conceive of space and the way they do the same to time. As far as space is concerned, there are those cultures which only give prominence to one aspect of space conceptualisation while others may uphold two or more levels of its (space) utilisation. In the former, space may only be used in connection with the satisfaction of material conditions of life while the latter may add a social function to it.

Time is also culturally determined. While the nature of relationship between time and culture is self-evident, the intervention of other variables may distort such a relationship. One variable that easily does so is the level of technological advancement which affects or is affected by culture and which could provide it with a completely different structure. The relationship between space, time and technology is clearly seen in Africa, South of the Sahara. Here live people who are different among themselves in cultures but which essentially have certain common features. The diversity in the cultures of African peoples to the South of the Sahara has been a basis for the conclusion that there is nothing common among the African cultures to warrant the view that there is a common conception of space and time. Using the conceptions of space and time as elements of culture, this paper investigates the relevance of asserting that there are certain common features in the cultures of the African peoples despite the diversity. The aim is to justify the view that there is something uniquely African which is shown by the common idea of space and time among the African cultures.

• Cross-cultural Differences

Some time ago, when I visited India, I was privileged to be invited by some leading Indian scholars to their homes to share meals with their families. During such social evenings, I came across a number of cases that gave me a glimpse into the inner workings of social life among certain Indian peoples. One such visit gave me the impression about the nature of Indian family life which appeared to me to resemble what I am used to in Africa, namely, that there are strong family ties which is characterised by unity among the family members. I noticed that several people (i.e. family members) occupied relatively small space and that the sharing of evening meals together in a family setting while talking is something which emphasises cohesiveness within the family. The members of the families I visited in India freely discussed with me and asked me several questions about the culture from which I come. In all such interactions, it appears to me that the centre of attention among these peoples is social relations, as evidenced by the fact that most of the questions I was being asked revolved around such things as family and kinship ties, marriage and other aspects of social organisation, arbitration of conflicts within the family, the role of religion and other normative belief systems etc. What I clearly noticed is that little attention was given to material conditions of life - such as whether or not people own cars, the types of houses our people live in, the salary levels of professors etc. I also noticed that some of the most prominent Indian scholars live modestly. They do not all own cars, or large houses and several other materialistic facilities. The impression that one gets is that Indian scholars seem to be more interested in 'high thinking and low living' since, despite the reputation of many of them in world scholarship, as shown by their great works, at home they live entirely unassuming lives: the houses and the spaces within them that they occupy are relatively modest.

The contrast is found in my other visit to the United States where I also had the opportunity to visit the residences of some American scholars. Here I was amazed at the great houses in which the American scholars lived. These are mansions or flats or apartments with several large rooms and extensive sitting rooms. During conversations I had with their family members in their presence I noticed that the discussions revolved around the material conditions and not social life as was the case with the Indians. They wanted to know whether we have cars, the types of houses we live in etc.

These two episodes are introduced here to illustrate the differences that exist between the Oriental and Western views of life. In the Indian case (which represents not only India but all people of the Third World), we see emphasis on communalism, while the American episode is brought in to show a focus on individualism. The difference has other implications of philosophical nature, namely, idealism and materialism. Moreover, the fact that the spaces within the houses in which the Indian scholars live have a lower ratio between the living and other spaces per person, as opposed to the higher ratio for the Americans, shows the differences in the conception of space between the peoples of the two worlds.

- Functional Conception Of Space

The differences between the American and Indian space utilisation also illustrate the two ways in which all cultures of the world could be broadly divided in their view of space. These two are the European or the West in general (as represented by the Americans) and the Third World (as represented in my example by the Indians). These two ways are mainly based on the functions of the space used by these people. While the Third World cultures have only one function for space, the West have two functions for it. For the Third World communities, space is used for living, for building or for such other direct functions which I here conceive of as 'Utilitarian'. For the West, space has both utilitarian and social functions. In the former case it has all conventional uses to which all cultures in the world use space, while for the latter it is a symbol of social status. An American builds a big house with large rooms not because he actually needs all those spaces for direct utilitarian purposes, but mainly as a symbol of social status; otherwise there would be no convincing explanation for a family of two or three to have an apartment or a house with six large rooms, besides the living room, kitchens and toilets. In this case, some of the spaces enclosed by those rooms would have no direct utilitarian value except that they are there to enhance the social status of the owner of the house. But, to the American this interpretation may not be strictly correct because he sees such 'wastage' of space as a norm provided by his own culture. This is why he is not unique in this respect and his fellow American friends who visit him will not notice anything strange in having such large amount of space for so little use. This normative convention is essentially rooted in the American culture as it is a part of it. If it does not manifest itself in the house, it comes into fore in other spheres. For example, the early American cars, which I regard as the traditional American cars were very large, when compared to the early Japanese ones. The differences in the sizes of the cars manufactured by the two nations essentially reflect the amount of space considered necessary on the basis of the relevant peoples' conception of space which is determined by their respective culture. Among the Japanese, it is not only that their original cars were small but the Japanese also build houses with small rooms (compared to the Americans), which reflected the need for immediate utilitarian requirements. The Japanese are a non-Western people as are the Indians and Africans. But they are as advanced in technology as the Americans. So here it is culture which is responsible for the differences in the conception of space and not levels of socio-economic conditions.

• The Conception Of Time

The situation is different in the conception of time. While some people see time in terms of fixed duration divided into hours, minutes, seconds and other smaller units, the majority of world's peoples see it in terms of approximations with little or no attention to precision. Here time is an element whose duration cannot be quantified. To some extent, it appears likely that the first way of viewing time is related to advancement in technology where there are precise machines for determining such a precision. Such societies are generally mechanised. But the mechanisation alone is not enough to provide a people with precise conception of time. It is culture which provides the background in the context of which precise measurement of time with machines can be determined. The role of culture comes in fundamentally because technology is an aspect of culture which shapes it. So it is a combination of technological advancement and culture which provide precise conception of time to a people. This, therefore, explains why Third World people's conception of time is markedly different from that of the First World (which include the technologically developed Japanese) mainly because most of the former are not as technologically advanced as the latter. There is, therefore, some justification for the First World peoples to designate particular conception of time as the 'coloured peoples time'. Most of the so-called coloured peoples live in the Third world and their skin colours range from the yellow of the Mongoloids all through to the dark or black of the Negro-Australoids. These are the same peoples in whose cultures the use of machines for time measurement is at its lowest. In most cases these people use the natural phenomena or astronomical bodies, such as sun, moon and other planets to tell time. Since calendars produced by different peoples on the basis of the solar system are culturally determined, the conception of time based on them is bound to be different.

Therefore, we have three levels at which time is conceived in the world. These are (a) time as viewed in the First World, (b) time as conceived in the Third World and (c) the intra-regional variation in the conception of time. The last one constitutes the variation within the First World and Third World views.

In the First World one can talk about the American time, the German time, the Italian time and so on. Although all these countries and peoples are technologically advanced, the degree of precision in the determination of time varies mainly due to the intervention of culture. Thus, at one extreme there is excessive obsession with precision such as among the Germans while at the other extreme there are the Italians who are almost as imprecise as many Third World peoples. Americans and other European peoples fall in the middle between these two extremes. Differences in precision about time among the less industrialised countries are also noticeable. But here the degree of precision varies with the extent to which people have been influenced by industrialised world. As is well known, most peoples in the Third World were either colonised directly or were strongly influenced in their cultures by the First World. The variation in the degree of time determination among these peoples would have been determined by the extent to which the Third World peoples' cultures were thus influenced. However, other factors come in to distort this possible unilinear correlations. The factors include the extent of the persistence of indigenous culture among a people. Thus, in the countries that were strongly influenced, there is confusion, which results from the condition of transition between foreign and indigenous cultures. That is why some among such people are strict with their time-keeping while others among the same people are relaxed.

• African Culture And The Conception Of Space And Time

There is a very big debate among scholars as to the nature of African culture. To some, Africa is merely a geographical expression that has no cultural meaning. This school of thought sees Africa as made up of Caucasian peoples with Islamic based cultures in the North while South of the Sahara has Negroid peoples whose cultures differ one from the other and upon whom had been imposed the Western Christian traditions. In such a diversity, they argue, it is meaningless to use 'African culture' as an expression of the cultures of particular peoples in that continent. Such an expression only makes sense in geographical terms.

The other school of thought, represented by myself (in press) and all the others that have used the term in a cultural context, there is what is called 'African culture' as opposed to the expressions 'European culture' or 'Oriental culture'. Each of these expressions implies certain levels of commonness in certain cultural elements that make up such cultures. Thus, the expression European or what others have preferred to call 'Western culture' or 'civilisation' has certain common features in belief system which is evidenced among others by Christianity, social organisation, such as marriage systems based on Christian culture, particular family structure which is dominated by monogamy and nuclear family; a system of writing, general similarities in material culture, etc. Within this commonness there is also diversity. For instance, although Christianity as a religion embraces a major part of the Western world, this Christianity itself is segmented into several sects (e.g. Catholicism, Protestantism and others) each of which in turn is further subdivided into other smaller units. Such variations within the European culture are almost endless. Yet, that does not prevent us from legitimately talking about the existence of European culture.

Similarly, the expression 'African culture' also contains certain commonalities in cultural expression. But here the expression is limited to the culture of the peoples of Africa, South of the Sahara and excludes North Africa because the latter has intrusive cultures that came in from the Middle East and made North Africa an extension of Middle East. Therefore, the expression 'African culture' embraces the cultures of the peoples who originated in the continent of Africa and who have remained in that continent barring the migrations of peoples and cultures from one part of that continent to another. The only peoples whose cultures qualify for this expression are the black peoples of Africa. They originated there, evolved there and are still there, although some of their kind have migrated into other continents where they form foreign population just in the same way as migrant Caucasians in Africa remain foreign to the continent, despite the antiquity of their migrations into Africa.

Having thus clarified the meaning and scope of the expression 'African culture', it now becomes clear that there are several common features in the cultures of the peoples embraced by the expression. This means that it is possible in broad terms to talk about the African conception of space and time, whereby the two concepts are seen as elements within the cultures of the Africans. This is particularly found in Africa's philosophical ideas in the form of legends, cosmology, cosmogony and generally in African belief systems (Mbiti, 1967; Jenkins, 1978). Everywhere in Africa time is generally measured in approximation, which is based on traditional calendar systems resulting from meticulous observation of the heavenly bodies. The results of such observations are culturally modified so that time and calendar systems, though common to all Africans in general, have certain variations in correspondence with the local differences in culture, sometimes under the influence of foreign cultures, e.g. the Ethiopian calendar which was influenced by the early Christianity and which provided it with non-African ideological influence, although the intervention of Ethiopian African culture provides this calendar with its uniqueness among the Christian based calendars.

Also unique to Africans is the conception of space. Here two issues are involved. The first is space as viewed in spatial terms while the second is the shape that such a space takes. In the former, Africans seem to compare with other peoples of the Third World as represented by the example already given concerning India. Here functional utilisation is the most important. This situation can graphically be illustrated by a functional analysis of the inside of an African house (Odak, 1986; 1988) and homestead (Wagner, 1970; Denyer, 1978). In the Luo house, for instance, every space within the house is put to specific social use and there is no space left in the house with no function. This is also true of the spaces enclosed within a homestead (Lang'o, 1997), so that the extravagant use of space as evidenced in European (i.e. Western) culture is drastically minimised. This is largely not because there is no available land for such extravagant use, but because of the economy of space as built into the African culture.

As far as the shape the space takes in African culture is conceived, there is the idea of circular or oval shapes. A study of the rock art of Africa shows that Africans have a tendency towards circular or oval shapes. According to Chapline (1974), African rock art seems to symbolise a system of thought which is based on the conception of circularity. This is not only the case with reference to rock art but also to all aspects of culture fundamental for giving a clue to the nature of the African system of thought. Examples can be found in the design of the material culture objects (e.g. circular stool chair, circular or oval design of shields, ornaments, etc.). This tendency towards circularity is the antithesis of the Western one where angularity constitutes the foundation around which the cultural system revolves.

From what I have said it is clear that space and time are the two common attributes of African culture. In time and space we see fundamental and, possibly, diametrical opposition between the African and Western or European cultures.

• African And Western Philosophical World-Views

Since the world-view a people have is part of that people's culture, the differences in the conceptions of space and time between the Africans and the West also presuppose the differences inherent in the cultures of the peoples occupying the two regions of the world. This is particularly so in the belief systems. European world-views are eclectical, involving religion and science both of which have created a type of epistemology that substituted object for the symbol and concentrated on the reification of the object with the accompanying devaluation of senses, excessive reliance on scientism and logic, the supremacy of the absolute, the abstract and the analytical, as well as the despiritualisation of the human. All these have been accompanied by the evolution of Christianity and of colonialism and cultural imperialism as its associative developments which were projected as a semblence of rationality. In the field of aesthetics, there was an attempt to impose a myth of universal aesthetics which is intertwined with the tyranny of rationalism (Ani, 1994).

On the other hand, African based epistemology has not substituted objects for symbols and not emphasised the object as opposed to the spirit. This means that religion in Africa had its own domain within the cultural system where its role is not subdued by any other aspect of culture. Hence, there is no alienation of the spiritual life by the abstract and analytical systems of thought. This distinction between science and spirituality based systems does not, in any way, subdue one element over another but provides a condition for complementary existence within a cultural system. However, the domination of the African by the European, resulting from slavery and colonialism and the spread of Christianity with its eclectic ideology, led not only to the confusion of the African in religious terms, but created a condition of helplessness which still is the order of the day at present. Nevertheless, there is currently an awakening of cultural nationalism among the Africans and a feeling that something has gone wrong. Such revivalism, which is occurring through imposition of cultural self-conciousness, creates a new platform from which to re-examine all the earlier paradigms in theoretical anthropological thought with a view to putting in place such alternative paradigms that are consistent with and arising from the cultural systems of the local peoples. Such a paradigm will inevitably examine different regions of the Third World and the cultures of their peoples, see what is common among the peoples and what is different and explain the reasons for such differences and commonalities. Afterwards, attempts would be made in putting forward a new alternative paradigm which explains those phenomena in the Third World that could not be adequately explained by the current paradigms, based as they are on the European systems of thought.

• Conclusion

The discussion of the topic has revealed that time and space are elements of culture. Since cultures differ from one another, there are also differences among the peoples of the world in their conception of space and time. However, despite such diversity, one can divide the world into the West (or First World) and the Third World, whereby the former, with respect to time, includes all industrialised countries. As far as time is concerned, the level of technology plays an important role in influencing how people conceive time.

It has become clear too that the Third World, as represented by India and First World, as represented by the United States, differ among themselves in their focus on human relations. While the first emphasises unity of the family and communalism, the latter is basically individualistic and socially disintegrative. Moreover, while the Third World focuses more on spiritual virtues as a factor in social life, the First is basically materialistic, despite espousal of Christianity which has introduced eclecticism (i.e. intertwined materialism with idealism) into spiritual life. Such differences are also noticeable in the conception of space. While the First World's cultures see space as useful in both conventional utility and provision of social status, the Third World has only one use of space namely, conventional utility. For time, the West gives weight to precision while Third World's conception of time is based on approximation. This difference is created by the variation in the levels of technological advancement.

Finally, I have noted that there exists an expression called 'African culture' which indicates a recognition of the existing common features in the cultures of African peoples. Such common features form the basis for the assertion that there exists the general African conception of space and time.

I have then concluded that the differences in culture among the world's peoples also presuppose the differences in the world-views, which calls for the formulation of alternative paradigm of anthropological theorising to that of the West.

REFERENCES

Ani, Marimba, 1994, *Yorugu : An African centered Critique of European Cultural Thought and Behaviour*. Trenton, N.J : African World Press.

Chapline, J.H., 1994, 'Prehistorical Rock Art of the Lake Victoria Region', in *Azania*, Vol. IX.

Denyer, S., 1978, *African Traditional Architecture: A Historical and Geographical Perspective*. London : Heinnemann.

Jenkins, D.V., 1978, *Ancient African Religion and the African American Church*. North Carolina : Flame International,.

Lang'o, D.B., 1997, Household Structures and Social Relations among the Luo of Ndhiwa Division, Homa Bay District, Kenya. A Postgraduate Thesis, Institute of African Studies, University of Nairobi, Kenya.

Mbiti, J.S., 1970, *African Religion and Philosophy*. London : Heinnemann.

Odak, O., 1986, *Shelter among the Maasai Peoples*. (Narok District Socio-cultural Profiles Report.) Nairobi : Institute of African Studies, University of Nairobi.

——, 1988, 'Traditional Houses, Their Internal Functional Division and Socio-cultural Practices among the Luo, Kuria and Maasai Peoples of Kenya', in *Collegium Anthropegium*, Vol. 10 (Supplement), I.C.A.E.S. Published Abstract Zagreb, Yugoslavia.

THE PARADIGM OF SELF-ORGANIZATION FROM VILLAGE TO PILGRIMAGE

J. McKim Malville

• The Benefits Of Non-Equilibrium

At one time, not so long ago, it was believed that the only stable configuration of matter, energy, living things and societies in our universe was that of perfect equilibrium, which is characterized by a detailed balancing of all processes. Since each creative process would be precisely balanced by an identical destructive process, it is really not a very interesting condition in which to live, although some people may prefer its stability and security. Equilibrium is a state of maximum entropy, with no surprise, no innovation. Perfect equilibrium is a condition of darkness, ignorance and death.

The physical chemist Illya Prigogine was one of the first in the West to demonstrate the thermodynamic and chemical benefits of non-equilibrium. He showed that non-equilibrium configurations can be stabilized through the export of entropy. As they move away from equilibrium, these systems may spontaneously develop complex structure and behaviour

We should not be surprised by such self-organized complexity, for we humans are complex, relatively stable and further from equilibrium than anything else that we know of. We are surrounded by complex non-equilibrium structures, ranging from stars to bacteria.

The biosphere of the earth is another example of a self-organizing system that has significant departures from equilibrium. Complexity has developed on the earth because it is an open system. We acquire high quality energy from the sun, are not so close that we are destroyed by its heat and export lower quality energy into the surrounding reservoir of interstellar space.

Many of the pilgrimage systems of the world are similar self-organizing systems in which complexity develops spontaneously through the free and autonomous actions of ordinary people in search of an ideal. Non-verbal communication between individuals and pilgrimage landscape may establish multiple levels of meaning.

- SELF-SIMILARITY

Self-organizing structures are characterized by self-similarity. Similar patterns are repeated with different sizes. With no fundamental scale or characteristic size, self-similar structures are unchanged after increasing or shrinking their size.

Pilgrimage systems are replete with self-similar structures. The pathway walked by the pilgrim may represent the entire universe from centre to periphery. The pilgrimage journey may mimic the entire age of the universe from beginning to end. Since they can be enlarged or decreased without changing their essential meaning, the geometries of pilgrimage, whether held in the mind of a pilgrim, drawn on the page of a manuscript, or embedded in a pilgrimage landscape retain their universal meaning.

The cosmic mountain that the pilgrim circumambulates may be both the universe and a temple; a change in scale does not change the essence. The *garbhagriha* of the Hindu temple is both the dark and watery womb of life and the point of creation from which the universe expanded outward from chaos. Circulation about the temple may be revolution about the cosmic axis, the motion of the sun in the sky and a spiral backward into the beginning of time.

Self-similarity is the key to the story of Shiva and Parvati asking their two sons to demonstrate their love by racing around the universe. Ganesh circumambulates his parents who are also the entire universe while his brother begins the immensely long journey along its perimeter. Both pathways are equally valuable and meaningful for the pilgrim.

- CHARACTERISTICS OF SELF-ORGANIZING SYSTEMS

Fundamentally necessary conditions for self-organization are openness to the outside world and non-equilibrium. Closed systems fall into the death of equilibrium, like a city, person, or planet enclosed by impermeable walls. Other characteristics of self-organizing systems are given below :

(i) *Openness* : Matter, energy and ideal must flow through the system, which must be able to add 'negentropy' or to 'eject' lower quality energy in order to generate complexity.

(ii) *Non-Equilibrium* : Equilibrium is a state of death. Detailed balancing of opposing forces prevents change and innovation. Only systems that depart from equilibrium can achieve significant complexity.

(iii) *Coherent Behaviour* : Isolated, non-communicating elements cannot achieve self-organization. Interactions between individuals are amplified by non-linear processes. Continuity and repetition achieve a cumulative effect.

(iv) *Resonance* : Cycles within a system can be coupled when they possess similar characteristic frequencies. When frequencies agree, power flows into the system and sudden transformations can occur. Resonance is a powerful means of achieving holistic behaviour.

(v) *Strange Attractors* : The system is dynamic and changing, drawn toward increasing complexity and transformation by 'strange' and unpredictable forces.

(vi) *Metastability* : When driven away from equilibrium the system may approach a threshold, similar to super-saturated saline solutions, in which small fluctuations may cause major and sudden transformations.

(vii) *Self-Reference* : The system develops without dependence upon external authority, stabilizes itself through internal feedback loops and creates its own meaning (teleonomy). Auto-catalytic loops energize the system.

(viii) *Symmetry Breaking* : Perfect geometries and exact symmetries have no uniqueness and no information content. Broken symmetries are necessary for surprise, variety and complexity.

(ix) *Indeterminacy* : Because new states are created by the amplification of small fluctuations, the outcomes of change are unpredictable. Self-organizing systems lack a goal or teleology.

- Fractals

Self-organizing, self-similar systems are characterized by fractal geometries, which have forms that are not those imposed upon us by rigid Greek views of geometrical beauty. Fractals are the free spirits of the world of mathematics and geometry. They are the natural objects of the world like the branching roots of trees, a braided stream and the coastline of Norway. They may have *fractional* dimensions, not just the 1, 2 or 3 dimensions of a line, rectangle or sphere. For example, the fractal pattern invented by the Polish mathematician Sierpinski has a dimension of 1.58. It seems but a small step to the self-similarity of the intertwined microcosm and macrocosm of the Sri Yantra.

- Power Law Distributions

Self-similarity of the large and small is expressed in power laws in which different sizes and lengths are united. In the Sierpinski fractal there are many more small triangles than large triangles. Their respective numbers are represented by a power law distribution, such that N is proportional to size raised to a certain power. Similarly, the variation of the size of structures in the fractal coastline of Norway follows a regular power law. A common power law for all sizes demonstrates the internal self-consistency of the fractal.

Such a power law distribution is a litmus test for self-similarity, for fractal geometry and for self-organization. A certain scale arbitrarily imposed upon a system would violate such a power law and stand out like a sore thumb. We find the distribution of the separation of the 108 shrines of the Panch Kroshi encircling Varanasi to have a power law distribution. The natural world is full of such power law distribution between the large and small : earthquakes in central America; the large and small natural disasters in North America also are related by a power law as are the words in the English language (Zipf's law).

• From Village To Pilgrimage Centre

The strangeness, novelty and unfamiliarity of the pilgrimage experience, its liminality using Turner's (1969) terminology, leads to the state of non-equilibrium and imbalance of the individuals. The catchment basin of a pilgrimage centre contains villages which themselves may be self-organized complex systems that depart from equilibrium, as has been noted by Professor Saraswati. The village may be brought to a state of self-organized criticality through what Professor Saraswati identifies as the bio-spiritual needs of the individual. Such bio-spiritual stress may drive the village community out of balance into a state of metastability. Resonance with the sun and moon may result in the movement of people at critical times of the year. The circulation of pilgrims from village to pilgrim centre creates an open space that transcends regional diversity and social stratification and opens up possible pathways for innovation and individual social mobility (Bhardwaj, 1973). Like the churning of the cosmic ocean to create *amrita*, pilgrimage stirs the cultural landscape, produces new life-giving options and prevents the stagnation of equilibrium.

The critical event leading to the onset of pilgrimage may have been a charismatic leader, a powerful individualistic vision, a miraculous cure, or a novel idea. A pilgrimage tradition may start when the cultural system departs sufficiently from equilibrium that a very light fluctuation can produce a transforming avalanche of spontaneous change and new structure.

Preston alludes to the 'spiritual magnetism' that draws people into a pilgrimage centre. Equilibrium systems attract like sink drains attract water and black holes attract matter, but there is a different kind of attraction in pilgrimage for there is no single, persistent goal to be pursued. The goal changes as the pilgrim changes and the journey may be endless. Changing dynamical systems can be described mathematically in terms of fixed point or 'strange' attractors. Closed systems moving toward equilibrium are drawn by a fixed point attractor toward a predictable end such as in the cases of the diffusion of a drop of ink in a glass of water or the gradual slowing of a swinging pendulum. The presence of a 'strange' attractor is an essential condition for the growth of complexity in a self-organizing system, as it is pulled into self-transformation by unpredictable, changing and ambiguous forces. There clearly are powerful attractors at work to cause pilgrims to journey far and undergo sometimes extreme physical hardships in search of an ideal. In its ambiguity and unpredictability the attractor of pilgrimage shares features with the strange attractor of mathematical chaos theory. In his description of complex 'physical systems' Cambel (1993 : 4) comes remarkably close to a description of pilgrimage : 'Complex systems are dynamic and not in equilibrium; they are like a journey, not a destination and they may pursue a moving target'.

- Resonance

One of the very powerful processes that can transform a dynamic system is resonance, whereby small fluctuations may slowly accumulate, if they are synchronized with other cycles and may produce major changes. The natural world is filled with examples of resonant behaviour that can produce system-wide changes, such as the destruction of the Tacome Narrows bridge, gaps in the asteroid belt and the holistic behaviour of the Galilean moons of Jupiter and the rings of Saturn. Resonance is alluded to by Paul Wheatley in his discussion of the symbolism of the city, when he speaks of 'an intimate parallelism between the regular and mathematically expressible regimes of the heavens and the biologically determined rhythms of life on earth...' (Wheatley, 1971). Most pilgrimage systems are dominated by resonant phenomena as people come into synchronization with fundamental frequencies of the world. Annual pilgrimage events may be experienced as ritual re-enactment of creation, which become more powerful as the number of participants grow.

Alternately, a resonance between humans and the heavens, repeated over millennia as may have been the case in the Nubian Desert of southern Egypt, when repetitive visits by nomadic pastoralists during the summer monsoons between 10,000 and 7,000 years ago established an incipient pilgrimage tradition at the Nabta, involving cattle worship and megalithic structures aligned to the sun and stars, which we have recently discovered to the west of Abu Simbel.

Pilgrimage landscapes are not the 'complex adaptive systems' that have been the focus of some recent archaeological modelling (Gumerman and Gell-Mann, 1994), nor is an adaptive dualistic, neo-Darwinian model even appropriate for these kind of systems. Adaptation is a response to something 'other' that has come into being by another set of rules. Self-organization is not a response to something outside that threatens, but includes the full range of the cosmos leaving nothing outside.

For an example of a complex landscape that bears the imprint of both pilgrims and kings, I turn to Vijayanagara and Kishkindha. It is dominated by a great north-south axis passing through Matanga hill, the most precisely established astronomical structure of the pre-telescopic world. It is a combination of natural landscape and kingly imperative. In addition, the landscape seems to have imprinted upon it the bow of Lord Rama. Matanga hill seems to be the source of creation and protection. Lines across the landscape trace the motion of time and the destinations of pilgrims.

• Conclusion

The complexity of the pilgrimage landscape may be natural and self-organized. We do not need to look for evidence of imperial decree, a city planner, pundit, or priest when encountering complexity in the landscape. The landscape may be transformed by a robustly open system that is holistic, complex in space and time and quick to change.

There is great depth to the landscape and the experience of pilgrimage. Let us not be deceived that the entry of mathematics, physics and chemistry into this discussion diminishes in any way the deep mystery of the pilgrimage experience. There is breathtaking mystery and grandeur to the fractal, which in its self-similarity continues inward to Plank length to the heart of the tiniest piece of matter and outward to its expanding boundaries some 15 billion light years distant. There is mystery and grandeur in the rising of sun every morning over the Ganga, greeted every morning by thousands of pilgrims on the west bank of the Ganga at Varanasi. But the deepest mystery is that these complex pilgrimage structures were created by ordinary people walking across the landscape in pursuit of an ideal.

REFERENCES

Bak, P., 1994, 'Self-organized criticality: A holistic view of nature', in *Complexity: Metaphor, Models and Reality*, D. Pines and D. Meltzer (eds.). Reading, MA: Addison-Wesley.

——, 1996, *How Nature Works : The Science of Self-Organized Criticality*. New York : Copernicus, Springer Verlag.

Bak, P. and K. Chen, 1991, 'Self-organized Criticality', *Scientific American* 246: 46-53.

Bhardwaj, S.M., 1973, *Hindu Places of Pilgrimage in India : A Study in Cultural Geography*. Berkeley : University of California Press.

Cambel, A.B., 1993, *Applied Chaos Theory: A Paradigm for Complexity*. Boston: Academic Press.

Coleman, S. and J. Elsner, 1995, *Pilgrimage : Past and Present in the World Religions*. Cambridge: Harvard University Press.

Gummerman, G.J. and M. Gell-Mann, 1994, *Understanding Complexity in the Prehistoric Southwest*. Reading: Addison-Wesley.

Jantsch, E., 1980, *The Self-organizing Universe : Scientific and Human Implications of the Emerging Paradigm of Evolution*. Oxford: Pergamon Press.

Malville, J.M., 2000, 'The Cosmic Geometries of Vijayanagara', in *Ancient Cities, Sacred Skies: Cosmic Geometries and City Planning in Ancient India*. New Delhi: IGNCA and Aryan Books International

Malville, J.M. and J.M., Fritz, 1993, 'Cosmos and Kings in Vijayanagara', in *Astronomies and Cultures*, C. Ruggles and N. Saunders (eds.). *Niwot*: University Press of Colorado.

Malville, J.M. and Rana P.B. Singh, 1995, 'Visual Astronomy in the Mythology and Ritual of India : The Sun Temples of Varanasi', *Vistas in Astronomy* 39: 431-49.

Preston. J.J., 1992, 'Spiritual Magnetism: An Organizing Principle for the Study of Pilgrimage', in *Sacred Journeys: The Anthropology of Pilgrimage*, A. Morinis (ed.). Wesport : Greenwood Press.

Saraswati, B.N., 1985, 'Kashi Pilgrimage: The End of an Endless Journey', in *Dimensions of Pilgrimage: An Anthropological Appraisal*, M. Jha (ed.), pp. 91-104. New Delhi.

Schroeder, M., 1991, *Fractals, Chaos, Power Laws : Minutes from an Infinite Paradise*. New York: W.H. Freemen and Co.

Wheatley, P., 1991, *The Pivot of the Four Quarters*. Chicago: Aldine.

PART III

EXPERIENCE AND EXPRESSION

9

DYNAMICS OF CULTURAL COMMUNICATION: ANTHROPOLOGY OF EXPERIENCE

S.C. Malik

• Language, Culture And Communication

The modern era begins with the 17th century when more so than ever before, in an evolutionary sense, the written word — language — with its other associations begins to dominate human behaviour. It reflects an overspecialisation of a distinctive area of the brain; the role of the cerebrum which consists of two distinct halves — each functioning autonomously in sorting out information received, i.e., the left side is more logical, rational and involved with the use of language; the right being more intuitive and syncretic. But when this integral development of the nervous system breaks down and the two halves do not exchange information and get severed for one reason or the other, then a dualistic or split personality is formed. This oppositional duality reflects the psychological state of man today; the neurotic life dominated mostly by the linguistic context, distant from authentic first-hand experience. All these developments suggest an overspecialization of the left brain. One of the most conspicuous indication of this functional asymmetry, or lateralism, is the phenomenon of 'handedness' — right or left (Malik, 1989, 1995a,b,c,d).

There are fairly obvious risks attached to a brain that operates on a double-plan system, the most outstanding being the danger that the two separate mental domains might vie with each other for control over the organism. Today, it is recognised that both hemispheres are involved in higher cognitive functioning, but there is a division of labour and fundamental modal differences between the two sides. The two hemispheres process information differently and are organised differently. It is not surprising, in view of the fact that they are separate entities, that they should have differing views of the world. In spite of their marked differences there is a modal complementarity in the functions of the separate hemispheres: one could generalise and say that the left tends to think in words and the right intuitively, holistically in images. The combination of the two systems are far more effective than one on its own. Even if one may see with one eye, our stereoscopic vision is essential. So also is stereocognition necessary to make us function holistically and express ourselves harmoniously and in a creative manner. This is the only way one may respond to a universe and nature which is similarly organised but one which may never be revealed except in its own style of dynamic functioning — in all its various dimensions (Fiumara, 1990).

Every individual brain is subtly organised in different ways, its psychic configurations creating unique patterns of ability and personality. Each individual psyche makes its own response to the inherent dualism of the mind/brain just as it responds to the cultural dualisms that are a feature of all social structures. In general these preferences are made as unconsciously as those of the left/right dominance determining reflex itself: we are quite 'naturally' of an artistic or scientific bent of mind, or for that matter, political orientation.

Thus, the divide between the East and West may also be seen, beginning with the 17th century, to be the dominance of the left brain activities as against the non-verbal, non-logical and 'fluid' methods of Eastern philosophies — the likes of which has disappeared in Western thought but are surprisingly perhaps making a return via the new vision of science itself. It is worth mentioning that psychologists have noticed that the left brain has a distinct tendency to 'take over' and feel itself responsible for all the actions of an individual, even to the extent of rationalising those decisions made by its right partner that it has played little or no part in making. There is surely an analogy in the functioning of modern society of rulers, political and other authority — the experts and their systems — who claim that they know what is best and have an overbearing attitude. One of the philosophical problems thrown up by the confirmation of the dual mechanism of the brain concerns the nature of consciousness. Modern science — relativity and quantum theory — has cast doubts on the nature of space, time, matter and energy which are no longer tangible, solid 'things'.

This brief introductory background is necessary in the context of the dominance of the Western mode of communication widely prevalent all over the modern world. The stress in this paper, within the context of the theme of the seminar, is on an integral approach to the understanding of these two kinds of knowledge — the holistic functioning of cultures.

Contemporary man has not given due importance to the negative dimensions of expressive language, which is easily seen by the domination media — whether newspapers or audio-video means. All these developments have led to a social behaviour which reduces the un-speaking, non-expressive other as a void, a negation. In many earlier non-industrial societies, the power of the unsaid was equally of crucial importance. We know that a large part of communication was carried out taking into account this 'unseen' aspect of the functioning of the brain which now has been lost in the use of mere expressive language — the constant chatter of the brain is the source of a great deal of anguish and sorrow for humankind.

The modern man and his philosophies are grounded in only half a language, i.e., within any discourse the strength of listening is ignored. In fact, what one takes to be a form of genuine dialogue, is mere speaking without listening. There is actually no authentic listening taking place. To illustrate, modern culture and society are working at hardware illustrated by the number of radios, TV sets and newspapers circulated. In terms of indicators of so-called development in the information-communication systems, it is totally ignoring a broad-base of human communication networks that are deeply rooted in the cultural milieu characterised by oral traditions which represent a continuous creation in the now (Finnegan, 1992).

Hearing basically implies hearkening and heeding and in this way listening is supposed to be a transportation of hearing proper into the realm of the spiritual. Obviously, in this sense it is not relished by a materialistic world. It is precisely this aspect of our culture that rationality has largely neglected. Today social scientists, anthropologists and folklorists are doing a rethinking on what they are doing and looking at cultures from this alternative approach within the context of oral traditions. For example, to examine events and processes; to speak of shared experiences as an important aspect of anthropological knowledge; and to see that integral listening means openness and a true dialogue.

However, modern culture's non-listening has given rise to two types of conceit, one of nations and the other of scholars who believe that what they know is as old as the world. The tacit, ubiquitous belief that recent Western logic represents the most reliable cognitive standpoint appears to characterise this worldwide modernism. Has not listening, as an ancient art, been gradually lost in the noisy inflation of discourse and by the infestation of pseudo-symbolic language? Or, conversely, could it be that the vital, ecological rationality has exhausted itself in its overwhelming production of talking and since it is more interested in hunting than in cultivation?

Has this intellectual heritage not caused the conceptual connections of other traditions to disappear? Has it not given rise to an idea of truth which is fitting for the vacuum it has produced?

In short, Western knowledge in this excessiveness of rationality and logocentricity, has left little room for listening. In fact, there is one voice only as the accredited source of knowledge, i.e., the celebrated science-power equation revealed in the coincidence of technological development and social-political hegemony. This is why unless listening, a part of this holistic approach, comes to be seen as a radical and valid point of departure, the biosphere will turn out to be uninhabitable. This is why a 180 degrees turnabout is essential and a change of route is worth the attempt at the level of world-views and philosophic foundations.

• The Mythic Domain

Myths arise out of a broad-base out of the collective unconscious. There are however many meanings given to myths and their nature; a debate has been going on for many millennia, which perceives myths as distorted memories of historical events, or as moral or psychological insights and so on. It is not possible here to trace some of these ideas in their historical setting. What one can say is that with colonial expansion new information was received about different peoples all over the world. By the middle of the 19th century, ethnologists and anthropologists attempted to deal with this new data in terms of some all-embracing new schemes of organization, viz. evolution of language, culture and mythology. In this way the early stages were represented by various indigenous cultures within some value-laden theoretical ladder wherein mythologies were seemingly irrational obsessions of these peoples and the ancients — a prelogical, as James Frazer said, mode of thought that did not allow them to distinguish between Man, Nature and Cosmos. Even later, Durkheim with his functionalist approach to myth and culture, explained it in terms of social function, customs and attitude rather than on looking into some deep philosophical meanings in myths. Of course, Freud viewed myths as primitive humanity's disguised expressions of unconscious sexual and aggressive compulsions. Both Durkheim and Freud who influenced most of the first half of the 20th century, sought to identify religion with illusion and explain myth by reference to physical, social or psychological phenomena. Later it was realised that something was missing in this collective dissection, analysis and classifications of myths.

Not universally, but many psychologists, anthropologists and historians have abandoned this reductive approach. This radical new way sees myth as a door to a realm of experience that was and is, both real and profoundly meaningful. Mythologies simply are not a study of economic, social and cultural meanings. In them lies the primacy of the sacred that is present in all traditions; and this is not present in any evolutionary order. These reveal and clarify their common motifs, a universal pattern is revealed, for example, rock, trees, rivers and clouds are parts of a whole in which the Cosmos is alive and conscious; it partakes of the same intelligent force by which humankind itself is animated and acts as a link between the inner dimension of spirit and the outer world of form. In this domain every individual knows that his/her life is the embodiment of a larger principle — norm, *rita* — so that even the most mundane activity has an overarching significance because every act is not performed as a personal private act but as part of a Cosmic drama. In short, the respect for the sacred is derived from an awareness of the creative process of Nature and it implies a hesitancy to arbitrarily intrude on those processes in which time and space are themselves sacred.

Almost all non-industrial human cultures in the past and even today have traditions belonging to this simple yet magical harmonious atunement with Nature and the Cosmos. There is a mythic unity in the spiritual and religious realms; for, repeatedly in America, Africa, Greece, India, Australia etc. cultures have pursued this Cosmic unity in varied ways both metaphorically and literally. It is a sacred world-view which lacks any sense of sectarianism or dogmatism because there seems to be an understanding of the universal order and meaning of existence that guides one in relationship to social order, Nature and Cosmos. Indigenous people have never assumed that Nature exists for the benefit of Man; rather humankind owes a responsibility to mother Earth and all its creatures — plants and animals. They, in fact, are apologetic for exploiting the earth for their food and clearly see the Universe as aware and benevolent. In this sense, there has been a decline of humanity, for religions of today appear as remnants of formerly universal spiritual traditions which had the original sense of a sacred purpose.

Modern science — physics — unlike classical physics is recapitulating in many ways the ancient spiritual world-view of integral living. But in these new formulations, is it possible to discern any sense of the sacred? And, whatever the name given to this ultimate source — this universal ground of Being — is no modern invention. Indigenous peoples all over the world were masters of holism long before this term was coined.

- **Convergence Of Modern Science And Ancient Insights**

Humankind today faces a crisis at many levels, despite (or because of) the magnitude of resources available as a consequence of tremendous technological and scientific growth. The idea of 'progress and development' begins with the positivistic-reductionistic, empiricist and anthropocentric enterprise in Europe in the 17th century.

Underlying contemporary challenges are certain unquestioned assumptions (e.g. rationality, linear time, subjectivity vs. objectivity, nature vs. man). Although outdated by Modern Science, these paradigms dominate decision-makers who continue to ignore many of the alternate world-views of indigenous-non-Western cultures which are very relevant today. This is the perspective of interconnectedness, simultaneity and multilayeredness of reality; of a seamless whole, a continuum in which we — earth with its creatures and the universe — are all enmeshed within a Unified Force-Field, Energy or Consciousness. This overarching energy-field is expressed in various cultures through the mythic domain within which experiencing takes place, allowing for the psychic maintenance of socio-cultural variations. This domain is crucial in understanding indigenous cultures; it is the source wherein lies our collective memory. Modern man has ignored this dimension at its own peril, although it is trying to create a new world order with the myth of history, the myth of materialism and the myth of science; believing as if together these will provide answers to all our prayers, to all our questions about existence. This seeking for answers about one's identity in externalities alone has increased desperation and alienation; it has encouraged revivalism and fundamentalism. Clearly, this myopic unidimensional viewpoint has brought upon us many diabolical scenarios for the planet and its creatures. Have not imagination and intuitive knowledge as experience, which is the essence of living cultures, taken a back seat?

The viewpoint suggested above may be disturbing since it challenges earlier frameworks and the unexamined certainties. The study of this area by many disciplines is inhibited by the essentially linear or non-contextual historical tradition that provides the presuppositions of scientific enquiry in the West. But these instruments of Western rationality are not applicable to other cultures, wherein rational principles are decoded through their own world-views, i.e., a text within its own context which is peculiarly non-linear or contextual. This is to be understood in the way complementary frameworks in Quantum Mechanics are created by different contexts of measurement — frameworks that are mutually exclusive (and therefore non-linear) but ordered to one another in a lattice structure (and therefore, complementary). Complementary frameworks involve changes in the embodied subjectivity of the observer. Knowing about cultures therefore cannot be done with the head, on the conceptual soil of Europe, nor can the new models be formulated about culture and development without sounding the death-knell of this culture and civilization which is still a living body. Lived experience of such cultures seldom arises by describing the surface of their world; this knowledge must act, reflect and communicate experience since it is this Consciousness of man on which man counts and man must get hold of it in himself.

The reference here is more to Western thought which has become a cultural determination for all men. The first determination, for instance, in the problem of the One and the Many, was the identification of the One with Thought; and the second that this Thought was Being. This notion has become common to the individual both in the East and the West; that is, Being identified with the word which proclaims in this fashion as able to control universal human behaviour, to this logic. But this will not allow us to reach the shores of other cultures which do not take Thought and Being to be identical. It is possible to understand these cultures through the action and meaning given in their cultural 'texts', implicitly and explicitly; abandoning one's own theoretical knowledge, i.e., the starting point will be that Thought is a subset of Being. The latter, for instance, is not an element in the conceptual system — it creates a reference to a domain of things, processes and events and it exists independent of any human involvement. Being is primal and as mentioned in Buddhist tradition 'What is evident— *pratyaksham* — to men is concealed — *paroksham* — to the gods and what is concealed to men is event to the gods'.

These ways of looking at the world may further be illustrated by the responses from philosophers of the West and the East, to the question 'What am I?' Socrates, as quoted by Plato attempts to bring together the 'what am I?' for the question by trying to figure out the X — what and thereby have the answer to the dictum know thyself. There would be a long list of each of the identifications given to the 'what' of man in the History of Western Philosophy — thus figuring out the identity of man or what it meant except were it not for existentialism or phenomenology. But in every answer provided, the phenomenon itself was forgotten as meaningless. In this way the 'what' became a strictly linguistic question, or some sort of an empirical problem which could be answered by adding up sets of empirically discovered characteristics or as a substance etc. In contrast, in other cultures, it is not the 'what' nor the subsequent possible identifications with the 'I' which would give an answer to the problem, but rather the AM-BEING of the question. What is being looked at is neither the question of identity nor even the 'I' as the source of enquiry but to go to the core of both the 'what' and the 'I', i.e., existence itself, the AM-BEING which every enquiring subject is before he even bothers to figure out the essences, or substances, whatever else becomes fashionable or to enquire about within a community. In the modern world this dictum has become a question of achievement, of seeking self-identity, personality through several frantic steps of one order of the other (de Nicolas, 1976).

The main point of this comparison is not to prove anyone nearer the truth than another, or to arbitrarily establish contact points between East and West. It is clear that man must realise himself as 'this', 'that', 'here', 'there'; since originally and finally man was able to become one or another or several in an infinite repetition of this first affirmation of existence-as-capacity. It functions as the original 'space' out of which all forms and names derive; as original space, it is the container of all human possibilities.

Thus, one can say that there are two sources of knowledge — one, the indirect one (called understanding, imagination, etc.) and the direct one (called sensibility, perception, etc.); the two sources of knowledge are called as 'non-sensuous' and 'sensuous' sources — neither better nor worse except in the manner of how we deal with the world. Instead of negating each other, these might be seen as complementary. In short, there are many ways of viewing the world and describing it without any one way being pre-eminent over the other. If this is not the case in the modern world, it is because of certain preconceptual visions which are exclusivists and not inclusivists and are adhered to dogmatically. The need is to transcend one's own framework. These two distinctive ways are available to man to view the world; the dominant 'commonsense-classical-physics viewing' and the 'Modern-Physics-Eastern viewing' of the world. Man's condition is such today that he is bound to use both viewpoints if he is to solve the problem of the 'real' nature of things.

Modern physics and the Eastern world-view assume that whenever we are in search of anything, we are primarily in contact with a totality, the most 'real' aspect of any entity being the 'total' pattern. Our perception of 'it' defies any atomicity or real identification. It is only secondary that classification of individual entities is made possible and for this we revert to ordinary symbolic manipulation. For example, one no longer says, 'Here is an electron' but says 'Here is an area where the field is strong'. In this view, 'what is' appears as a quantum, a whole, a totality; the identifiable parts of this totality are artificially created for purposes of linguistic communication and conceptualisation: they are artificial sub-patterns. The separation is totally false in relation to 'what is'.

The impact of this idea is to note that we are living in a continuum, in the present, where the distinction between the living and dead, between moving bodies and bodies at rest, etc. no longer holds good. Man is now in nature, not seeing something distinct from himself. In this way we shall have to describe things in new and better ways; sometimes creating and selecting or abstracting. The human condition is such that both ways are essential if man is to feel at home and this is what complementarity means. 'It is not that there are songs to be discovered but that the symphony was already there — sometimes in one note or in one song because both are necessary in knowledge'. This freedom is necessary if one wants to stop reinforcing what one already knows. The historical accident of the discoveries of quantum mechanics and their relation to linguistic communication, complementarity, indeterminacy and vision, makes our project of understanding cultures easier.

- Anthropology Of Experiencing The Other

Perhaps the greatest shortcoming in cultural studies is the hidden presupposition that our linguistic criteria are the only ones by which all men and cultures should be measured or reduced — the positivistic view of language where the logic is universal irrespective of how the people use it. It is essential therefore that we do not presuppose what culture is before we discover it. Culture is always incomplete, always on the move; this gives it a certain indirection as an open phrase hanging in mid-air.

The knowledge we formulate about the 'other' is filtered or refracted through the knowledge we have built for ourselves, i.e., we are interpreters of cultures and can observe the 'Other' only through our own cultural and experiential biases. But this is not all so subjective, for at any given time there are accepted norms of what knowledge is conceived to mean, i.e., the knowledge of the 'Self' and of the 'Other' come together in terms of some subjective and creative understanding; say, about new sights, sounds, rhythms, silences, feelings and tastes amidst many other cultural paraphernalia (Hastrup *et al.*, 1994). This does not mean that language is not important in that culture and that they are not linguistically sophisticated. It is just that in the natural flow of interaction, especially in music and dance and so on, there is something behind the words — a hum of another kind — which takes into account a large sensory inventory which cannot be frozen into the written word that becomes the so-called ethnographic record. The human approach to a cultural model must encompass all 'experience' even if in terms of categories — taste, smell, sound, shape, colour and so on. Moreover, while linguistic categories may be gradually learnt, cultural learning may just have to be picked through sheer participation — doing the right thing at the right time, by feeling something beyond language that give some meaningfulness and vibrance before these are classified and explained away. One can of course only attempt to approximate to the verbal and non-verbal experiences in terms of the shared experience and as far as possible it is to share emotions - if at all in any case. Maybe there can be a lived understanding of the situation, event and process.

We need to consider our model along these lines; the multiplicity of perspectives. Modernism has imposed a single perspective in dealing with human language and human culture. Cultures have to be seen as a whole, linguistic or otherwise. It is to see the presuppositions and criteria on which life is ground, to discover a different way of viewing and listening. This perspectival vision thus does not rupture the continuum between thought and action, viewing and action. To reduce and measure man by the image of his thought carries inevitable consequences. For one thing, what is not an image a thought, is outside of man, a mystical power, a god or a devil; while whatever is human must of necessity be only that which appears or is an image. For another, the only possible role for man to play in a world grounded on thought is to systematically reduce and control all his possibilities to the reality offered by the image; it is to condemn man to a programme of desensitization. The integrating way to see this in many cultures is to put an axe to this tendency, so that all perspectives are kept alive simultaneously.

It has been overlooked that most social experience about cultures lies beyond language, both 'theirs' and 'ours'. Cultures are not things, objects or theoretical frameworks. The error lies in the production of anthropological-ethnographic-knowledge which has ignored experience — personal and social. Language categories fragment the experience of both the 'self' and the 'other' i.e., there is an inherent unidimensionality and linearity involved in this domain of objective rationality which blocks out experience (subjectivity and intuition). The contention here is that this need not be so in any exclusivistic terms as both domains are crucial for understanding cultures in general and specifically in India.

Clearly, the spoken or written word involves one of the senses and not the other senses (say, smell, touch, feelings, sight, rhythm and so on) which express vividly what cultures are all about, especially Indian civilization. It is dominated by oral means of transmission of heritage where songs, music, dance, poetry — the arts in a broad manner — are important. The first step is to rethink earlier axioms and assumptions of the research involved. An awareness of the issues and seeing that such fusion is possible between the two poles, is itself an important step in contributing to methodological frameworks. The verbal and the non-verbal encounters merge into a continuum since often minimum words are needed in this form of communication. The emphasis is on the fact that the total representations of the senses in understanding other cultures or representing them is crucial. We may call this as knowing the taste or essence of the culture and a removal from that spatial ambience does not replicate the same essence of this aspect of culture — it is out of context.

In short, over and above the intellect, linguistic utterances, the full range of bodily sense — experience — is an important means for approaching others' experience — beyond the linear, preordained format. It is not implied here at all that the linguistic means is therefore redundant or subordinate to this form of knowing. One may call this grounded knowledge, a most appropriate medium available which has been disembodied in the name of objectivity.

Understanding other cultures is only possible when they are experienced comprehensively; the internalisation of the holistic social and cultural experience is crucial since it allows one to move beyond conceptual worlds of people, to a totality that comprises thoughts, feelings and emotions. In fact, this is the only way which allows for a fuller understanding of both cognitive and embodied knowledge. Understanding cultures is not about information categories, it is a learning process that can only come via experiencing. This is especially true for India.

• The Context Of Rita In The Rigveda

There are many ways of viewing the world and describing it without any one way being pre-eminent over the other. The need is to transcend one's own framework, this creation of pseudo-problems through an idea of 'either/ or' framework, taking the atomisation of language and its separateness of the things of the world as real: subjects and objects, man and the world, agent and re-agent, observer and the observed, life and physiology, mind and bodies, self and the other.

Rigvedic man (other such cultures) refused to create new problems by separating the inseparable and searched instead for that other way of viewing the world which happens as a result of transcending common sense language and its viewpoint. The point is not of having a philosophy but articulating philosophy beyond a single set of possibilities and liberate man from these various controls, inner and outer.

This is not only a way of viewing the world but one of interacting with it; making freedom possible by falsifying all controls through the knowledge of the controls themselves. The positivistic view of language along with its own ground of meaning has to be dropped and the researcher has to be free from this belief. This freedom is necessary if one wants to stop reinforcing what one already knows, for example, the achievements of a method that allowed fixed notions about nature, society and the individual. But there is the absolute falsification of this method, since we find ourselves trapped in a continuous crisis of nature, society and the individual. However, while the crisis of nature does not bother us too much, the crises of society and the individual hit us closer to home, where it hurts. This is where man's fourth dimension comes in, where critical philosophy and meditation coincide.

Cultures thus have to be seen as a whole, on two points at least: (1) the conscious ordering of the structures of experience and (2) the dynamic activity produced through the conscious ordering of these structures. It is to see the presuppositions and criteria on which life is ground, how through structures and the activity based on metaphysics, ontology, logic and epistemology etc. are combined in order to discover a different way of viewing and listening. This perspectival vision thus does not rupture the continuum between thought and action, viewing and action. In short, the basic structure of this situation is then a human consciousness, consisting of both a subject and a field of objects, towards which the consciousness is turned intentionally.

From this perspective, every movement is the whole, the whole is in every movement. This is the fully realised presence of a total system of possibilities embodied in every movement. In presupposing a field opened by sight, for modern man, vision came to be based on a linear kind of movement, which disclosed a perspectival, three-dimensional space and linear time. In contrast, in the *Rigveda*, the audio space-time structure opened by sound was articulated not only by rhythmic and cyclically recurring movements, but movement itself became the base of all contexts (structure).

and the source of meaning within each and every field of experience (de Nicolas, 1976).

Thus, the integrating way is to see that all perspectives are kept alive simultaneously. The implied philosophical activity, say in the *Rigveda*, holds that the internal language of images is essential to both human experience and human progress in such a way that both become dependent for their functional efficacy on a clear understanding of the language of the images themselves. The rishis of the *Rigveda* resolve the philosophical activity of integrating different images by means of the language of the sacrifice, a sacrifice of complementary integration which leads to new creation through sharing in an effective way of viewing human action (*dhih*) according to the effective body of common law or norm (*rita*).

The *Rigvedic* mind was certainly not after abstract definitions of essences. It was worried about what existence really meant, the concrete act of existing; and the observation of this act was their whole concern from the *asat* to Vision. It is the 'sheer-being-able-to' that takes the name and form of the existing actuality.

The main point of this comparison is not to prove anyone nearer the truth than another, or to arbitrarily establish contact point between East and West. It is clear that man must realise himself as 'this', 'that', 'here', 'there'; since, originally and finally man was able to become one or another or several in an infinite repetition of this first affirmation of existence-as-capacity, which is the *asat* of *Rigveda*. It functions as the original 'space' out of which all form and name derive; as such, i.e., as original space, it is the container of all human possibilities.

For Western readers, this again might be understood, this space, as some 'visual' model leading to a visual synthesis of their human experience as is common when speaking about 'vision', including sense of ears, mind, eyes etc. that one reads into the language. But are we dealing with a 'visual' model or of an 'audio-aural' model? The vision spoken here has nothing to do with looking, but the model is grounded on 'sound', not 'sight' (de Nicolas, ibid.). Western philosophy from Aristotle downwards, has equated vision or contemplation with gazing at human life from the heights of theory; the soil of vision and contemplation has remained theoretical. The only form of transcendence possible within such determined confines is either, the dialectics by which the process of executing theories is accelerated, leaving in its wake a world empty of human creation but uniformly nominalistic.

On the other hand, in the *Rigveda, asat* is a tonal context ruled by the criteria of music, the ground of transcendence, the origin of all organised perception, the original ground any and all sounds count on in order to sound. It is simply silence that embraces a whole spectrum of sound, from its absence to its plenary confusion. The flesh wants to be music; for this was the beginning. Sound emerges as all of organised sensation and of all communication; sheer vibration, energy, possibility — the sounding silence from which the worlds, gods and man emerge, is the space of discourse. But modern man has deprived himself of the possibility of returning to his origins and that of others. This is the only sin path of *rita* could not tolerate, for it deprived man from the eternal return to his origin and tried to reduce the multiplicity of embodied-songs to one theoretical voice. Contemporary man and contemporary science, especially psychology, needs to dwell on this sin; for unless memory and imagination are freed from the theoretical constraints limiting their movement, man and woman cannot recover their body completely. Not allowed to reach the beginnings of the human body we all carry with us, the present crisis of contemporary man and woman. The *Rigvedic* insight needs not only verification but to recover our own act of creation and the power to revive it. 'We have forgotten the Dragon, the Snake, the Silence and the Flesh that wants to be music' (de Nicloas, ibid.).

If one does not agree with this view then one is agreeing to the method of the natural sciences, as the only method whereby man and his 'body' may be understood, explained, predicted and controlled. A necessary condition of the method is that in experimental observation one variable must be constant: the 'body' as an organism must be conceived as historically resting, while the mind may be conceived as historically moving. Even if the approach to the study of body has changed with improved instruments, it still implies that we have better explanations of the body than before, while it stays unchanged. The idea of predictability and control is facilitated by this notion, which is repeatable. Hence the idea of behavioural control or genetic manipulation is the result of this journey. The historical man is thus denied human freedom of creation, of freedom which present day education inhibits completely. The memories of body buried, imaginings and rhythms are unable to be released.

Western and Eastern scholars, have tried to attribute a visual model to the *Rigvedic rishis*, on such a presupposed visual model as the synthesis of their sensorium. It is commonplace that man's sensory perceptions are abundant and overwhelming; but it should be equally evident that it is impossible for man to attend to all of his sensory perceptions at once. Every man is part of a civilization which is committed to an organisation of the sensorium stressing certain types of perceptions and neglecting others. This may be a telling clue about specific cultures — historically speaking — that any given culture is committed to one prominent way of sensory perception and that their way is not necessarily ours, is at the root of many of our misunderstandings and misinterpretations of other cultures. This Western 'visual' culture is at the worst odds to understand and interpret a culture like the *Rigveda*, where the stress is not so much on the visual, but rather on the oral-aural. There is in this field of exploration a sensorium synthesis in the *Rigveda*; it is at once varied, vast and intricate.

It is obvious, when talking about the whole human-sensorium, that this refers to the world of sight, sound, taste, smell, touch; the relations of touch to sight and to sound, the relations of those sense perceptions to our expressions in the vocabulary of our vernacular, the relations of those sense perceptions to our self-identification and to the perceptions of others, i.e. interiority and exteriority. What might not be so obvious is that a synthesis based on sound as a primary model of organizing sensation contains a multiplicity of perceptions that will certainly have a different character from, say, a synthesis based on primarily sight-perceptions alone.

A society bent on sight-perceptions and on the fixedness which such a priority in perception carries with it, is mostly concerned with surfaces, with objectifying, with fixed spaces and with objects in such spaces; a society so perceptually inclined cannot stand the light, but only its reflection.

In the *Rigveda* then, there is sound, which is the greatest key to interiority among all of our senses, even though interiors of a certain kind are also felt through touch and kinesthesia. But it is only through sound that interiors as interiors are manifested. Sound is the greatest clue we have to interiority, our own and that of others. It is only sound which makes true interiority communicative.

Sound discovers interiors by invading them physically; the hearer vibrates not merely emphatically but in physical bondage (resonance) with the sounding body. Sound is absolute presence; it is an activity rooted in the present. Sight may provide a lot to think about, but it is only in sound that all the thinking is done. No wonder that sound, the word, has been attributed with power, even magical power. In this way the *Rigvedic* culture which stresses sound as the primary organizer of sensation, both sensation and thinking will have a different structure than the same process in a culture which stresses the visual. No thought or object is sensed or thought in isolation, but within 'sets', 'group', 'horizons', or simply contextual structures. The root of contemporary man's crisis is that while his culture tries to reduce his body to simply the names of an organism, contemporary man's body still remembers its origins in sound and refuses the nominalistic amputation (de Nicolas, ibid.).

By focusing on the criteria of sound, the measures of the structures of the language of Existence (*sat*) are discovered in the *Rigveda*. It would appear that the *rishis* did not have the atomization of names and forms in mind; but rather, the establishment of an effective activity centered at the heart itself of that powerful *maya* (force), originator of any and every activity; and which moved according to the norm (*rita*) through song (*vac*). Therefore in the *Rigveda* and by the silent criteria it presupposes, the act of creation is not a single, definitive act; but rather, an act which is repeated at every sound point.

There is also the world of touch, sight, taste, smell, etc. These are the multiple perceptions of structuring of the world in terms of the human body. Today psychiatry sees the appearance of multiple personalities as a threat to reason and has therefore labelled it as sickness; monotheistic personality has always been the prototype of modern culture and a *fortiori* of psychiatry — schizophrenia — at a time when whole cultures are being fragmented into multiple personalities, in painting, music, literature and even the natural sciences. The fragmenting personality polymorphs into numerous centres of spontaneity, relativity, discontinuity and disorganization. We were not trained to survive without the monotheism of personality and are unable to cope with psychological polymorphism, except as an excuse for punishment and control.

In the *Rigvedic* context, the existence of fragmentary, autonomous systems is not only acknowledged, but no social life is possible without them. However, a polymorphic personality allows for the condition of survival when one of our psychic centres cannot hold and things fall apart. Polymorphism in the human body is a psychological response to the challenge of breakdown and disintegration; it is a model for integrating disintegration. But this psychological aside cannot be easily understood in a culture ruled by the criteria of sight. *Rigvedic* methodology draws its main clue to interiorizing all perceptions, the whole sensorium from sound, which found the model of complete, absolute instantaneity and communication in sound. In one way, it was the instant way to become the total presence and power of absolute and efficient communion. While the other sensory media provided discontinuity, sound gave the eternal presence. The total presence of speech and the discontinuity of sight are both reconciled in the common origin of sound, through *vac*. This process presupposes an internal activity that is much in opposition to the Western activity that is suggested by the Western model of sight. Realizing the intimate unity of all existence, *Rigvedic* methodology tries to recapture it in an auspicious moment of inspired vision (de Nicolas, ibid.).

On the model of sound and by its criteria, the *Rigveda* offers us a completely different picture. The space is the musical scale and it is neither here nor there prior to song; space and song are simultaneous. Time, again, is not prior to the singer and the singer is no other than the song; the singer's body shares its dimensions with the structure of the song. The human body is polymorphic, multiple personalities as the body becomes the multiple perspectives it sings. Since the body remembers all its previous incarnations and since the human body was born in sound and ruled by its criteria, its therapy does not lie in submitting it into psychological monomorphism, but rather in releasing its lost memories, its silent music: the human body has the right to innovate and maintain continuity.

In the *Rigveda*, the individual, the society, the cosmos at large, are not three different entities, even though related, but rather society, cosmos and individual are all one body. This embodiment may be changed, modified, enlarged, made smaller, but in no way can it be radically gotten rid of. The effort of those same 'seers' was directed towards building such a common body as would make human existence most communicative, pleasurable and likable.

The *Rigvedic* philosopher-poets were very much aware of this 'tacit' dimension, i.e., the structure of subjectivity is the structure of the embodied perceiver, the subject. Different kinds of sense perceptions were understood simultaneously and were seen as influencing each other's growth. The distinction between both ends, subjective and objective, was understood by the *rishis* as an apparent discontinuity — time, brought about by the sensorium itself and its discontinuous perceptions. These ends could be re-gathered in a continuous efficacious instant-moment, a space, by falling back on the infinity of an organising force, underlying — and found inside of *nitya* — all discontinuity.

In summary, there are three main clues that guide one in the *Rigveda*:

1. A unitary and indivisible originating power — *maya* — moves in

accordance with the movement of the Norm — *rita* — and appears wherever the chant sounds — *vac*.

2. This coincidence of power, norm and chant occurs at any sound-point, any pitch being possible tonal centre for any kind of tonal structure.
3. God, heroes, dragons etc., are only the prototype — *pratirupa* — and the embodiment of multiplicity of perceptive — *purarupa* — generated from a common origin — *sayonih* — the musical octave, conceived as a field admitted many alternative structures (i.e., 'tuning systems').

Thus the movement of the *Rigveda*, the trajectory of its path, is pointing straight at the heart of the stillness; for the path of the *Rigveda* is none other than the power to still what moves and set in movement what is still. All this only may be known through meditation so that the human body is transformed. It is time to still the mind, historically moving for so long; time to set the body in motion, which has been historically resting for so long; let it become music again.

REFERENCES

Finnegan, Ruth, 1992, *Oral Tradition and the Verbal Arts*. London.

Fiumara, Gemma Corradi, 1990, *The Other Side of Language — A Philosophy of Listening*. London: Routledge.

Hastrup, Kirsten and Peter, Hervik, 1994, *Social Experience and Anthropological Knowledge*. London and New York: Routledge.

Malik, S.C., 1989, *Modern Civilization — A Crisis of Civilization*. New Delhi: Abhinav.

——, 1995a, 'Matter is Consciousness', in *Prakriti*. New Delhi: IGNCA.

——, 1995b 'Holistic Science and Consciousness', in *Prakriti*. New Delhi: IGNCA.

——, 1995c *Re-conceptualising the Science and the Humanities —An Integral Approach*. New Delhi: Manohar and Nehru Memorial Museum and Library.

Malik, S.C., 1995d, *Interface of Science, Consciousness and Identity*, (Forthcoming). New Delhi: IGNCA.

de Nicolas, Antonia T., 1976, *Meditations Through the Rigveda — Four Dimensional Man*. New York: Nicolas Hays.

10

UNDERSTANDING A CULTURE EXPERIENTIALLY

Anjali Capila

• Introduction

It is a truism that the foundation of scientific research is the search for objectivity. The 'objective' approach is an attempt by the researcher to be clinically detached and dispassionate in observation and analysis. How far this is possible in humanities is not clear. The drawback of this form of perception is that it atomizes phenomena under investigation and is a selective and isolated vision of reality. It removes from purview a whole range of other perceptions: for example, the worlds of wonder, of aesthetics and ethics. It may not be far wrong to state that this fragmentary approach, which ignores the 'subjective' aspect of being human, especially when it comes to investigating human societies, has in many ways been the cause of modern civilization's current state of alienation and loneliness and of the violence that is so widely prevalent today (Malik, 1995).

In view of this state of affairs, researchers in many parts of the world have begun to ask now to humanize the method of understanding human societies without demolishing the merits of science, rationality and objectivity. Attempts are being made to find ways of allowing us to inter-relate many of these layers in order to achieve wholeness. It is within this overall interconnectedness that the idea of participation arises — each part, each one of us participating in the totality. Participation is implicit in the wholeness of the 'participatory universe'. Nothing would exist if this was not so (Skolimowski, 1994).

• The notion of participation

Without elaborating on the philosophy behind the 'participatory universe', it is clear that participation is at the core of social life, it is the song of joy of individual experience. It is these experiential moments of oneness which bring richness and meaning into our lives. It is this song of life, this song of participation, which is amply illustrated by the women of Garhwal in terms of both individual and collective experience. It was possible for the researcher to learn and appreciate the significance of this approach through her own participation in the lives of the women she studied; and, conversely, through their participation in her life. This is the approach, the core methodology of this paper : the setting up of clear guidelines for an approach to field research whereby new methodologies may be evolved.

Deep participation means empathy, an almost complete identification with the subject of one's attention. Empathy or identification is a crucial aspect of participation, since it is what gives meaning to wholeness, i.e., empathy necessarily implies responsibility, which can exist only when there is participation on the whole (Skolimowski, 1994). To illustrate, the women of Garhwal spontaneously show a high level of participatory ecological responsibility not only for their environment but also for their families, households and areas of social interaction. It is this multi-layeredness that may be deciphered in their songs, provided one has the ability to move behind the explicit to the implicit experiential knowledge embedded in them.

It is in this sense that the songs of women become crucial and important source material for understanding the images and life-style of the women of Garhwal. It is this approach that can look at the material evidence that is central to their life. Central to our understanding of a culture are the notions of empathy, participation and responsibility. All these form a circularity of wholeness, in terms of flowing into each other, one partaking in the meaning of the other. This perspective is radically different from the 'normal' linear, 'objective' approach of the social sciences. The latter, from this researcher's viewpoint, is only a kind of 'cold' act, since it tends to treat human beings as objects within a linear methodology. However, the connectedness of isolated entities may also be observed within the context of the participatory model (Seth and Capila, 1988).

Participation is a process which allows for creative intervention. Now, the question which may be asked is: How does one translate these general insights into specific methodologies? How do we create a new rationality woven around the central concept of participation, in order to learn the new methodology? The way the songs, the 'material', have been looked at in this paper, provides very significant answers in terms of the new directions: that is the goal of 'participatory' research programmes. This approach is very appropriate for India because here cultural traditions are largely transmitted by oral means.

Some of the main prerequisites of participatory research are:

(i) Empathy.

(ii) Communion with the object of enquiry.
(iii) Learning to use the language of the 'other', literally and metaphorically.
(iv) Communicating with the 'other'.
(v) The ability to penetrate from within, in-dwelling in the 'other'.
(vi) Learning the ability to transform one's consciousness so that it becomes part of the consciousness of the 'other'.

Someone may be sceptical of these guidelines, especially minds trained in the rigours of 'linear objectivity'. It needs to be pointed out that this approach is not so difficult as it sounds, since most of us in our personal lives know, feel the sense of participation with the other. For instance, all of us know the experience of loving and being loved; the experience of personal pain which enables us to understand the pain and anguish of others; the deep experience — communion — with works of art, songs and dances, music etc. which allows us to in-dwell in that oral, audio-visual world which is beyond texts and words. This common sense everyday knowledge — experiential and conceptual — really has deep metaphysical meanings. It is to empathize and become one with the other, it is to beat the same rhythm with another, it is to understand through compassion and from within.

Again, some may point out that these vague emotional responses can only lead to a fuzzy methodology where nothing specific can be validated. In this research, terms such as in-dwelling, empathy, looking at things from within, all are crucial because they allow one to show how a new kind of dialogue becomes possible between 'subject' and 'object'. The wider implication is that in a general sense humankind today needs to carry on a compassionate dialogue between cultures and communities and also with plants, animals and the environment.

Bearing the above in mind, the questions which this researcher evolved, in terms of intellectual strategies — meaningful, rational questions — and new sources of imagination, were:

(i) What ought to be revealed and in what language?
(ii) How am I to evolve an ongoing dialogue?
(iii) At what level, in what forms and terms is this dialogue to be maintained?
(iv) How do I come close to the kind of sensitivities which the other embodies and operates through?
(v) What are the range and limits of sensitivities which I need to evolve in order to establish true rapport?

(vi) How do I translate all this into my own academic and non-academic terms and then into inter-subjective terms?

In short, how does one make the transition from 'objective' consciousness to compassionate consciousness? The integral approach presented in this paper is an initial attempt to provide inroads into these new areas. It is time that the social sciences moved into alternative modes of inquiry. However, the rational and the intuitive, the rational and the compassionate, are not antithetical to each other; at a deeper level of analysis, they are aspects of each other.

Participation implies the development of manifold sensitivities, so that wholeness is revealed in the multifariousness of its participation — part in the whole and whole in the part. One may call this holistic thinking, ecological thinking, one which transcends the boundaries of objective thinking. Its purpose is not only to acquire objective pieces of information but to heal, to maintain well-being and to enhance life, to make life more vibrant and radiant. This paper is an attempt to show that reverence for life is an integral part of being a human.

• Fieldwork And Experience

While it is true that knowledge is embodied in words, most social experience lies beyond language. For example, processes — experience of both the 'self' and the 'other' — is difficult to render in words (language categories) which, by their very nature, fragment and break up the reality they seek to represent. There is an inherent unidimensionality and linearity to language, because in emerging from its supposed objectivity and rationality it blocks out another kind of experience, subjectivity and intuition. However, the contention, as stated above, is that this need not be so in any exclusivist terms as both domains are crucial to any kind of understanding and, in fact, go hand in hand.

There are serious methodological problems not only in the context of what constitutes theory of knowledge, but also those which face the fieldworker seeking to arrive at an understanding of 'other' cultures and societies. The route from field experience to the formulation of analytical results is not an easy one. The value of fieldwork cannot be underestimated, because it is a crucial process whereby knowledge is produced. It is clear today that there is no sharp distinction between objective and subjective knowledge, between theory and practice or empirical studies which were once taken to be self-evident. But these distinctions, which arose out of scientific knowledge of the external world, are no longer valid in the sciences.

Until recently, the experience of the researcher in the field was reluctantly dealt with, since what mattered most were 'objective' analytical results, a kind of straight narrative-description of 'those' people by 'us'. These distinctions (valid only as categories of deconstructed objective entities) are no longer absolute as before, since the observer and the observed are closely linked, i.e, one's biography merges in the process of knowledge production.

One must be clear that subjectivity and experience are not secret and hidden, mystifying things, that cannot be shared, understood and communicated. In understanding creatively women's images in such an area as folk songs, the methodological shift from structure and function to process and events is exemplified. The holistic view of multi-layeredness or multi-levelness in horizontal and vertical terms, must be borne in mind. This is especially the case in understanding creatively women's images in their songs and associated activities, which is the particular focus of the many-faceted society of Garhwal. Thus the contextual shift from the static (pattern) approach to a dynamic (process) one is very significant.

• Participant-Observation: Lived Experience

The above in some ways refers to what is involved in the idea of participant-observation. The reference is also to what may be called lived experience, which is a prerequisite for obtaining relevant information during fieldwork since the non-verbal has to be experienced, participated in and performed, so to speak. The examples given later on, with reference to close proximity at many levels, are by no means an undue romanticization of participation in exotic worlds (as they are likely to be misunderstood by some). But clearly there are limits to what one can actually share and communicate with other people — which remark may hold true for one's societal interaction as well.

The issue of participant observation involves a high level of sensitive awareness, allowing little room for preconceived notions about the 'other'. It involves a reflectivity in which there is also a shared reasoning, an attempt to see logical connections within integral terms, since just saying 'I saw it myself' will hold little water. It is what one may call a shift from implicit knowing to explicit understanding. This is important because otherwise even if one were able to fully record all that was going on audio-visually of the 'native', it would tell us nothing in terms of contribution to knowledge. For example, in our case the goal is some form of coherent understanding, some causal connections between the different strands within the culture (Hervik and Kastrup, 1994).

The linguistic and the cultural models are interlinked in the actual behaviour — 'lived experience' as stated earlier — of both parties concerned. What one methodologically does in emphasizing experience is start from the idea of dialogue between the contact of the two — the 'self' and the 'other' — en route to the production of knowledge process, which is the goal of the researcher. Cultural models and categories, one discovers, have to be experienced comprehensively, if only to understand the practices (images, in our case) and motivations of one's self and the other. The internalization of the holistic social and cultural experience is important in this interpersonal realm, since it allows one to move beyond conceptual worlds of people to a totality that comprises thoughts, feelings and emotions. The researcher believes that understanding cultures is not merely about information categories, although these may later on be useful for other purposes, it is a learning process that can only come about by participatory experiencing. Every fieldworker has of course been acutely aware of the discrepancy between what is observed, participatively or otherwise and what is recorded. Reiterating the significance and the emphasis of this approach is an integral aspect of this study of women's images as reflected in songs.

• Functional Importance Of Participant-Experiencing

It is clear that experiencing allows one to understand different notions of events and processes; the latter are to be seen as a flow, like life. This is what is to be seen in the various categories of songs that reflect inner experiences which form the very core of lived and the shared culture of Garhwal. Someone may doubt this statement, to question the idea of how much of experience can truly be called shared experience. But some insight and creative understanding are possible through empathy since being in the shoes of the 'other' is almost an impossibility. The centrality of the methodological issue is on how to deal with this flow of inter-subjective human experience without dehumanising it as has been the case in presenting cultural models in terms of 'objectivity'.

Once this proposition is accepted other avenues do open up. In this way it becomes possible to come closer to discover many ways of representation of 'other' cultures. For example, in Garhwal, songs of women reflect group identity and the notion of female bonding. 'Her' song is 'our' song — such is the tremendous sense of identification by women of all ages and groups, especially when it comes to songs reflecting longing for the parental home. This feeling links all women, since it is a felt experience of 'longing'. This 'lived' experience is not taken to be something restricted to the personal self as in modern societies. There is both empathy and sympathy for this common feeling of longing which is shareable since there are no hierarchies involved at this level, no boundaries to transgress. The experience itself unifies the women into a universal whole.

What is significant to note here is that the study of folk songs is not one of seeing these as objective entities for mere analytical purposes. The latter is crucial too at one level for contributing to a body of knowledge. But the emphasis here is that all this knowledge has to be integrated within the experiential dimension both for the researcher and in understanding the 'other' culture. Folk songs are thus events and processes that are part of a larger whole of the total culture, interwoven within various manifestations into the very fabric of the life of the women. To illustrate, folks songs reflect a world-view and the women-centredeness of that society. Folk songs help us to understand a community and its life and act as powerful indicators for looking at women's lives particularly and the culture in general. Thus, in the community under study, songs are a part of a living — lived — experience, a tradition which is created anew in the immediate present and replicates everyday. It is an expression of one's being, of one's experience in day-to-day life. While it is transmitted through generations by word of mouth, the creator or experiencing person breathes new meaning into it. Singing by memory or recall through rote is more than just rendering of the song.

What one experiences personally is the 'lived experience', an aliveness of the song and its words which alone tells one of the lives of the women. How this is to be translated into knowledge is another crucial question since the written word is to be supplemented with audio-visual means even if that will only slightly approximate to the experience felt in the field. It does not tell one about the sense of identification which the women feel with the song. The women are not mere passive receivers of another form of entertainment as in modern times. They are active participants and the researcher herself becomes a participant-observer in this sense because the lived experience invokes, evokes and provokes something inwardly. It is in this sense that the study of folk songs for understanding women's lives takes on a significant dimension.

• Social Experience And Knowledge

As stated above, the knowledge we formulate about the 'other' is filtered or refracted through the knowledge we have built for ourselves, i.e., we are interpreters of cultures and can observe 'others' only through our own cultural and experiential biases. But this is not all so subjective, for at any given time there are accepted norms of what knowledge is conceived to mean, i.e., the knowledge of the 'self' and of the 'other' comes together in terms of some subjective and creative understanding; say, about new sights, sounds, rhythms, silences, feelings and tastes amidst many other cultural paraphernalia. This does not mean that language is not important in that culture and that they are not linguistically sophisticated. It is just that in the natural flow of interaction, especially in music and dance and so on, there is something behind the words — a hum of another kind — which takes into account a large sensory inventory which cannot be frozen into the written word that becomes the so-called field record (Kohn, 1994).

The human approach to a cultural model must encompass all 'experience' even if in terms of categories — taste, smell, sound, shape, colour and so on. Moreover, while linguistic categories may be gradually learnt, cultural learning may just have to be picked through sheer participation — doing the right thing at the right time, by feeling something beyond language that gives some meaningfulness and vibrance before these are classified and explained away. One can of course only attempt to approximate to the verbal and non-verbal experiences in terms of the shared experience as a participant-observer and as far as possible to share emotions. May be there can be a lived understanding of the situation, event and process. Primarily, 'I must feel and learn to express my own experiences'. The point that is being made is that in most fieldwork reports the early experiences and feelings of the worker tend to be forgotten, at best confined to reflexive introductions. The methodological question remains, how can the fieldworker make her experiences of the 'other' accessible if words do not do justice to them? Different media are necessary and the relevant tools and techniques for it, since lived experience is the stuff of art, poetry, music, songs and so on.

The content of culture, which we learn about through our experiences with others, is much more than what we can confine to texts - our learning is much more than a textual interpretation. 'We cannot live other people's lives and it is bad piece of faith to try...we can but listen to what in words, in images, in actions, they say about their lives, objectifications, discourse, performances, whatever we encounter', says Clifford Geertz (Kohn, 1994).

REFERENCES

Hervik, Peter and Kirsten, Hastrup, 1994, *Social Experience and Anthropological Knowledge*. London & New York: Routledge.

Kohn, Tamara, 1994, 'Incomers and Fieldworkers: Study of Social Experience', in *Hervik and Hastrup*, op.cit.

Malik, S.C., 1995, *Reconceptualising the Sciences and Humanities — An Integral Approach*. New Delhi: NMML and Manohar.

Seth, M. and Anjali Capila, 1988, *Studies in Communication*. New Delhi: Deptt. of Community Resource Management & Extension, Lady Irwin College, New Delhi; funded by UNICEF.

Skolimowski, Henryk, 1994, *The Participatory Mind: A New Theory of Knowledge and of the Universe*. Penguin.

11

DANCE AS COMMUNICATION WITH THE COSMOS

Yolotl González Torres

There are several paths for attaining spiritual experience, communicating with the cosmos and worshipping the supernatural. A very ancient and common one is dance which is also a 'part of many subsystems of belief about the universe that deal with the nature and mystery of human existence and involves feelings, thought and action' (Hanna, 203).

The power of dance in religious practice lies in its multi sensory, emotional and symbolic capacity to communicate. It can create moods and a sense of situation in attention-riveting patterns, by framing, prolonging or discontinuing communication. Dance is a vehicle that incorporates incolate ideas in visible human form and modifies inner experience as well as social action. The efficacy of dance in contributing to the construction of a world-view and affecting human behaviour depends upon the beliefs of the participants (performers and spectators), particularly their faith in their ability to affect the world around them (ibid.).

Dance may also be meaningful in itself in terms of sensitivity and perception : The sight of performances moving in time and space, the sound of physical movements, the odour of physical exertion, the feeling of kinaesthetic activity or empathy and the sensation of contact with other bodies or the dancers' environment (ibid. 204).

Dance as a religious practice has much to do with the culture's conception of the body, especially concerning emotion and sexuality.

Dance played a very important role in the ritual of the ancient Mexicans. We shall refer here only about the dances performed in Mexico Tenochtitlan, the capital of Mexico as we possess the most abundant data about them. During the 16th century previous to the time of the coming of the Spaniards, Tenochtitlan was the biggest city in the Americas, with very few inhabitants, with buildings and gardens which caused the admiration of the Spanish. It is my belief that in greater part of the rituals performed by the Mexicans, their main goal was to have a more personal communication with the supernatural. Dance was not the only means to attain their higher state of consciousness, there were several means. One of them was fasting, another blood letting from different parts of the body, ingestion of hallucinogenous plants and anointing of substances made of venomous plants and animals. Most of these paths to achieve higher states of consciousness were used by priests, shaman healers and chosen youths, but all the people had to fast and offer their blood in sacrifice and dance and sing. The dance was used as a sacred, ritualistic offering to appease the gods which thereby, imparted religious merit on the dancer:

Macehualiztli, properly means to deserve it, *macehualo* means to merit; they took dance as a meritorious task, in the same manner as one says to work for merit in charity, penance and other virtues. These dances were very solemn and they were performed in the general feasts and those of the gods. They used to dance in the plazas. With these, they not only called and praised their gods with songs of the mouth, but also of the heart and with the senses of the body, for which they had and used many ways with the movements of the head, of the arms and the feet and with the body they strive to serve their gods (Motolinia Memoriales, p. 136. Marti).

Ritual dances, as far as we know, were always a common affair. There were no individual dancers, or special temple dancers like the *devadasis* of India. I think that there have been very few cultures where such dance demonstrations took place.

There were very strict rules to follow, according to the deity who was honoured, as when to dance, who and with whom, to what type of music, songs, choreography, steps, movements of the body, type of costumes, body paint, ritual preparations like fasts or bloodletting and so on.

Ritual dance had to be followed so carefully that if any mistake was made by a singer, musician or leader of the dance, he could be punished with death, as the great energy which was expected to be generated by the dance and music was believed to lead to the communication with the cosmos and any mistake would produce a failure with it.

Most of these rituals were held during the solar calendar of 360 plus 5 days, divided in 18 months of 20 days, which were dedicated to several deities. All rituals including dance were controlled by the State through the priestly organisation and the ruler himself. There was one particular priest in charge of organising the ceremonies, but it was also the duty of the king himself to organise some of the dances and also to appoint the men who would lead them as well as the musicians. He would thus say :

Listen, this is your office
take care of the drum and the rattle.

You shall wake up the people
and give pleasure to the owner of the universe.
Through this medium you shall search this interior design
and you shall have it in your hand.
This is the way to ask and look for the Lord.
(Segal, p. 180, Cit kupryn p. 55)

The nobles were also conscious of their duty to be aware of the proper performance of the dances, so the parents admonished their sons 'to take care of the dance and of the drums and the rattle and of the songs, with these you shall awake popular people and you shall give pleasure to our God who is everywhere' Sah.I, VI, 17.(cit Marti).

There were two types of dances, one for enjoyment, called *netotiliztli* and one dedicated to the gods called *macehualiztli*. We shall deal only with the last one. The musical instruments which usually accompanied the dance were a vertical drum called *huehuetl* and a xylophone made of wood called *teponaxtle*, flutes, rattles, conch shells and raspadores. Good musicians were highly valued. Unfortunately all the music of those days is lost and we only have the numerous musical instruments which have been discovered in archaeological sites.

Dance was almost always accompanied by songs, but these as well as the movements of the dancers were under the lead of the instruments. Two people sang a verse and everybody responded. Usually the music started in a grave tone and the singers followed in low voice. Little by little the compass was fastened and they raised the voices becoming more joyful according to the song (Clavijero).

Dance could be performed in several places, but the usual one was the main central plaza in front of the Great Temple, where the images of *Huitzilopochtli* and *Tlaloc*, gods of war and water were placed, or in front of the temple of the god whose ceremony was being celebrated. It is said that around 400 people could gather to dance in the main plaza.

The scenario according to the descriptions and few of the paintings of the *codexes*, most have been absolutely impressive. The site was already sacred, but with the music, the presence of the living images of the gods, all the dancers dressed in their finery, made a sacred circle. The centre of power was occupied by the musicians and the king when he danced. The interior circles were formed by people from the upper strata in the social hierarchy who danced in a lower tempo, while in the outer circles the dance was faster.

In every dance a particular group of people participated — peasants, hunters, feather or gold workers, midwives and medicine men and women, merchants, warriors, administrators, young women, old women, prostitutes, noblemen, the king and so on, according to the type of ceremony which was being celebrated. The time when the dance was held also varied according to the ceremony. It could be in the morning, in the afternoon or in the night, according to the god who was worshipped.

There were special houses called *cuicacalli*, the houses of song, where the youths, male and female were trained in singing and dancing. The temple also had singers who were paid to compose songs in honour of their gods.

Dance also had an important role in sacrifice and the future victims participated very actively in dance.

There are many descriptions in the chronicles of the dances that were performed during the different ceremonies in honour of the gods. I shall describe only one or two to give an idea of its importance.

They gathered in a great circle, two by two or three by three, according to the number of people, they carried flowers in their hands and wore feathers, they made at the same time a movement with the body, feet and hands... all the movements went according to the sound played by the *teponaztle*. With this they went all singing with great concern and with sonorous voices, praising the god who was being celebrated and they still do it now... all very gracefully and very mystical...'(Clavigero ?).

In a dance in honour of their tribal god *Huitzilopochtli*, two groups of dancers were organised. In one of them were all the girls dedicated to his temple for a period of time, as well as his priests, apparently making two circles. The girls had their cheeks painted and the arms and legs decorated with red feathers, they wore a crown and a sort of band across their body made of popcorn, in their hands they carried maize canes with a black banner made of paper or of cloth at the top. Women's dress was a skirt (a tied cloth to the ankle) plus a loose blouse which was the common dress of women in Mexico. It only varied according to class and occasion. In this particular case the musicians were not located at the centre of the circle but inside one of the common houses called *calpulli*.

Another group of dancers was composed of the young and old warriors and the people of the palace, including women. The formation was made of one man and one woman, holding hands consecutively. They all wore their best, especially the warriors who had fabulous head-dresses made of feathers and precious metals. This dance lasted till night and it was guided by a man who was the living image of the god *Huitzilopochtli* and he was going to be sacrificed the following day.

All these dances took a long time, in most cases. In most cases there had been previous fasts, bloodletting, sometimes eating hallucinogenous plants, plus the odour of the *copal* (incense) and of the bodies and the blood of the sacrifices, plus the physical exercise of so many hours of dancing and the deep belief in the cosmic presence made it very easy to get them into a state of consciousness which allowed them to fuse with the cosmos and enter into another order of existence.

We shall now talk about a similar pattern followed by dancers today in several Indian communities. They are imbued by the same cosmic pattern as in their traditional religious dance, which is no longer performed today because of changed circumstances. Few decades back the participants were members of marginal communities of towns of Central Mexico. Some scholars like Gabriel Moedano think that it was born as a crisis cult and with great influences of the Otomi Indians; on the other hand many scholars think this dance has little to do with pre-Hispanic dances; other, especially nowadays, believe that it is derived from those dances.

The myth of origin of this dance ritual goes back to 1531, few years after the conquest of the Spaniards of the Aztecs and their forceful conversion to Catholicism. Fights were still going on against the pagan Indians. During one of these fights between Christianised and pagan Indians in a town named Queretaro, there was an apparition of St. James and a brilliant cross in the sky, after which the pagan Indians became converted and shouted '*El es Dios*', he is God and started worshipping through dance. This sentence has become a ritual sentence and a sort of mantra and form of salutation for all the dancers, who are commonly called *concheros*. They are called so because of their musical instrument *concha*, shell, which is a sort of mandoline made of the conch of an armadillo. We do not know much about the history of this movement but through a very patched oral history we can reconstruct that in 1800 they were organised in a sort of brotherhood, quite similar to the present one.

We know that around 1947 there were about 50,000 *concheros* - 10 percent in the city of Mexico, the rest in the states of Queretaro, Guanajuato, Mexico, Tlaxcala, Puebla and Morelos. Most of the *concheros* were masons, craftmen, small vendors and peasants who had migrated to the cities.

They are part of a brotherhood which links them in a ritual relationship. They are organised in communities called *mesa*, table, who consider themselves descendants of a common dance ancestor. The founder or *palabra*, 'rod' is represented in the flag or standard which they carry and is considered a relic. The *mesa* is also the domestic altar covered with a table-cloth embroidered by the Catholic images venerated by the dancers, like the Lord of Chalma, the Holy Child of Atoche, the Virgin of Zapopan and so on. On the top they also place the instruments of the *conchero* ritual : censers, bells, candles, flowers, standards, musical instruments and so on.

The organisation follows the Spanish military hierarchy : generals, captains, sergeants, *alferez* or standard bearers, soldiers and aspirants, plus two posts especially for *Malinche* women. *Malinche* is a purely Mexican character and strangely is the name of the woman who helped the Spanish with the conquest of Mexico and she has as her duty to carry the censers. The generals are the leaders with more prestige. The captains are usually descendants of the founder of the *mesa*, therefore their position is usually hereditary and can be held by a man or a woman. They are the ones who know all the rituals, the music and the myths and usually they are healers who have knowledge of medicine and plants as well as of the esoteric. They organise and lead the members of their *mesas*. They pay most of the expenses for common meals and other needs of their communities. They are in charge of calling all the dancers every time they have to attend a dance or a wake or *velada*.

When a dance is going to take place on the day of the festival of the saint in question, they gather very early in the morning in the atrium of the church. Then they go to the captain's house where they have a meal. After this they put on their costumes which differ according to the group, which have now become quite similar to the pre-Hispanic ones - men wearing ornamented loin-cloths, a clock and a sort of breast ornament.

After the dancers finish dressing, the captain nominates the first word, who is an elderly person, in charge to lead the ceremonies during the day. The third word shows the different steps and movements of the dance, the *Malinche* is in charge of the censer. When all the nominations are made and accepted they say '*El es Dios*'.

Then follows the march or walk to the shrine, which is already part of the dance. They form two parallel columns, headed by the standard of each *mesa*. They are accompanied by the *malinches*. At the head of the columns usually go the dancers who play the *conchas* or mandolins, after them the dancers with their ankle bells and hand rattles. The captain, the children, the old men and the *huehuelt* or special drums are placed at the centre and are thus protected by two columns. They go to the altar where they kneel down and sing a prayer and when they leave the shrine they walk backwards with respect.

When they reach the place where they are going to dance they form two spirals and then a circle. The drum is placed in the centre, where it is going to be played. The *Malinche* goes to the centre and gives the censer to the captain who salutes with it the four directions several times, while the rest of the dancers kneel. Then the captain places the censer in the middle of the circle. All the dancers mark a cross with their feet : up, down, in front and behind, to one side and to the other. This is the triple cross, tri dimensional, which places them in the centre of the universe. Before the dance starts they sing the following song :

To the battle my general
you who carry your holy light
Let share four halves
so that the cross is very well formed.

Gonzalez says that the battles are fought by individuals and groups. That each dancer has to battle against the tendencies of human nature which handicaps the internal attitude to act correctly the ritual and to reach estasy, necessary to reach the divinity or the divinity to reach them. On the other hand the communal fight is against the negative cosmic forces which may try to stop the ritual. The dancers form a battalion which strives to reach the light and make them their own.

When they finish the dance they return to the church and thank the image of the saint and retire. After that they have a common meal at the house of the host.

The general pattern and organisation of the dance are quite similar to what we read about the pre-Hispanic dances and there is no doubt that these dancers as Gonzalez says and as there are some other instances that prove that this dance is meant to get into communication with the supernatural, not to be possessed by a spirit or a god but just to reach a state where communication is made possible.

REFERENCES

Cupryn, Teresa, 1992, 'La expresion cosmica de la danza azteca', in *Revista Mexicana de Ciencias sociales*. No. 147, Mexico, UNAM, pp. 35-52.

Gonzalez Torres, Yolotl, 1996, 'The concheros, an ancient ritual dance in ancient Mexico', in *Bulletin of Urgent Anthropological Research*. ICAES: Vienna, pp. 69-71.

Sevilla, Amparo, 1990, *Danza, Culturey Clases Sociales*, Mexico.

PART IV

QUESTION OF UNIVERSALITY

PARADIGMS OF NEXT CENTURY

Rafael Lopez-Sanz

Today is a moment — an 'experimental moment', according to Marcus and Fischer (1986) — when, the salient paradigm of social sciences shows the fading away of the unnatural concept of 'utopia', giving way more and more *non-sequitur*. This is accompanied by a redeeming, spiritual mood which is like a sacred game. The new approach looks at technology and magic with new eyes and the old outlook on science and man, finally seems to have reached the boundary of chaos and perhaps, will dwell in Hades for centuries to come. *Nihil est.*

We can expose this in current, contemporary terms. I totally agree with James Heisig in his opinion that the idea — and the fashion, I will add — of the 'global village' (born and promoted since the writings of McLuhan and others) is not more than a 'virtual reality for those who count themselves its ranking citizens'. As Heisig sees it from Japan, following the case of the remarkable philosopher Tanabe, or as it is seen from a 'Latin American' country (this last an unreal globalized term) as Venezuela, belonging to the 'global village' has much the same meaning as 'internationalization' or 'cross-cultural communication'. These are, I agree, messages that 'make experiential sense to the community of 'internet users', especially when this community is inherently unconscious of such a global interconnectedness, being the result of what in fact MacLuhan himself knew. The new technology is apprehended 'as simply an improved version of earlier machinery', as Heisig says. More over this argument is worth supporting if it benefits the people of 21st century. This is McLuhan's proved proposal of understanding media as extensions of human mind and body, in time and space, and of this being 'the cornerstone of morality in the global village', as Heisig recalls which equals Tanabe's 'waking up to absolute nothingness as the basis for the absolute interconnectedness of all persons into a single human community' (Heisig, 1995: 13-14).

To further express this I want to bring here the antithesis of almost any Western utopia. Quoting a letter of Nishida, another great Japanese philosopher, to a friend, Mutai Risaku, the Mexican theologist Agustin Jacinto Z., from the Michoacan School, brings to us : ... 'In a World (westernized) in which there is no correspondence between the obnubilated (man) and Buddha, how could it come about what we see in the Buddha and the call of the Buddha. .... in the logic of the topos — topos is here used as 'figure' or 'images'; not as properly located places, real or not — the Name of Buddha results from that which is immanent = transcendent as its self-expression. This is why, by believing in the Buddha and the invocation of its name we are saved. This is not to contemplate the Buddha or something like it. As (the Buddha) cannot be contemplated only his Name is invoked' (Jacinto, 1995).

Well, one can detect that this kind of consciousness pervades man everywhere; it highlights a salient paradigm of today i.e., the paradigm of differences and complementarity which is expanding more consciously all over the world.

Today the paradigm of difference, complementary and conflict, acts strongly. It has substituted the previous one; showing signs and symbols of the life and activities of people of all places, a *non-sequitur*. New mythologies, music and rituals are making breakthroughs as expected in a cosmopolitan culture; linking New Physics with the old, little know Western traditions. Its energy is so vast that it has reached a quite non-clear, non-monotheist and non-monogamous phase of 'The World System': globalization, is rapidly expanding throughout a depleted planet. To me, this lies behind Ilya Prigogine's reflexive words after noting Durkheim's, Levi-Strauss's and Leach's contributions to societal models: 'What has been constructed by the previous generation shows everywhere in the form of exchange flux, which induce to restart the historic precedent constructions' (Prigogine, 1993: 57-59). That is, there are no defined structures and orders; there are transitions, processes and renewed attempts of more complex ways of comprehension and existence'.

To this I add that this sort of evolutionary feedback, as it is called by Prigogine, shows in us a peculiar, pertinent flowing consciousness of diversity, with the always strange Other and the multiple histories and lives that are without central power. Relating oneself with some postmodernists one could agree with Agnes Heller's statement that postmodern consciousness is the consciousness of modernity, and has created diversity (Heller, 1997).

Apart from the fact that the single destructive and collectivist experience of the 19th and 20th century men, a clearly modernist experience, should be enough to mark the scandalous end of the pretensions that today mark in their one way and language the boring globality via 'new technologies'. We have already said in previous statements that there is the hermeneutical demonstration of Mircea Eliade about the key role played in the modern culture and civilization by the religious dialectic form '...sundering from God together with the impulse of returning to the origins (the eternalized return) after the interreign and the correlative apocalyptic mediation — which the modern people call wars' (Lopez-Sanz, 1997:100).

I reiterate that this movement, essence of the worldwide and modernist history, that by the way is no longer only of the known Western world, with its antipode postmodernism, has produced the science Anthropology; and, with its nuclear movement around the topic of the time-lost-but-recoverable, since Malinowski to Levy-Strauss, to that seemingly unsuspecting anthropophagical ethnography, certain consciousness of which one captures in exceptions like Marshal Sahlins and Valerio Valeri. It is for this reason that answer to the questions like 'Recoverable?'; 'What could be Recoverable?'; 'Recoverable for what?', one looks for the traces of the utopia and its disasters. This is what made science and the power-holding majority, speaking in a defensive light, pronounce ethnography as non-ecologist. I highlight that ethnography is assumed here in both, its positive sense, aware of the real sacrifice and of its way towards culture *per se*, and in its cannibalistic sense, so contemporary, so daily, as the mirror of the manipulated consumer. Products and performances like the extraordinary one of Anthony Hopkins in the film *The Silence of Lambs* are more than a proof of this aspect.

Returning to our current Anthropology crisis, which has asked in the last three decades questions about the privileged status of Ethnography. While it is true that such a scene helps to understand better what the extraordinary work of George W. Stocking qualifies as 'a general failing of ethnographic will', it has shown many tendencies and 'programmatic manifestos of the mid-1980'. And I will agree with Stocking that this does not amount to the paradigmatic status that 'the Kinship system or the life-cycle did for earlier generations of ethno-graphers' (Stocking, 1992: 368-69).

Further more, from a 'Third World' point of view academic Anthropology registers with delay 20th century men's anxiety and phenomena already announced and treated by Joyce, Conrad, Eliade, Bateson, Adorno, Lezama Lima, Jung, Saint-John, Pense, Blake, Black Elk and many others. These have become contextual focuses and sources of reflection for the current, contemporary modern – postmodern tension. A drama and dilemma tensions that one finds again in the New Physics, in day-to-day life, especially around the re-dimensional role of a vital group of topics for today's man, mainly with regard to Time and with regard to illusion — a theme worth another essay, and an unending one — the Self and the Other, relativity, complementary, mutation, the mutable, and the Maya-Gaia subjects.

I formulate this delay as connected to the sort of limbo anthropologists lived with the ethnography moment, in times of Colonial diaspora, which in this current, neo-colonial moment, is linked to the anthropophagic ethnography cited above. Due to this, they are not quite alert to the new ways of being and existing around the planet reflecting now the complex, academic scene and a world that Stocking (1992) and Kuper (1994) have so well exposed. But one sympathizes if one sees it today: The intermediate moment formally registering re-inventions, present currents and themes of deep concern. An example of this lack of attention and of the 'general failing of ethnographic will', is today's numerous re-constructed Others, 'including, more recently, the fragmenting ethnic identities of the post-communist world' (Stocking, 1992: 372) (A new 'Third World'?). One should realize that this was just the human complexity foreboded in ethnography.

Finally, the above leads to a third derived paradigm, which we may now call an open-conflict paradigm. It has been internationally recognized that the explosive, complex and surprising contemporary scene triggers anxiety, violence, desire and new ways and types of coexistence all over the planet. From our 'Third World' position one views these aspects as rich kin-heirs of a vast ethnographic and ethnological experience, virtues willingly constructing a mediating way as interlocutor-translator between indigenous people and passions fighting cultural borderline and situations of crisis. This was especially so since our training in UNESCO-MEAD Institute seminars in Caracas, 'Three Brains for Peace', led by Elaine Beauport, Sofia and Enoe Texier. Whichever path one takes it should be taken with feelings and nostalgia of the virtues and deepness of the great monk Hsuan-tsang (596-644) (cfr. A.C. Yu, 1977) on his slow and long trip from China to India; virtues and depth that I suspect could offer us keys to understanding how it was possible with the appropriate slowness, to build a first, real and historical bridge between the bases of the Millennial West and the bases of the Millennial East.

REFERENCES

Connor, Walker, 1994, *Ethnonationalism: The Quest for Understanding.* Princeton, New Jersey: Princeton University Press.

Docherty, Thomas, 1994, *Post-modernism: A reader.* New York: Columbia University Press.

Eliade, Mircea, 1977, *No Souvenirs.* New York: Harper & Row Publishers.

Heisig, James W., 1995, 'Tanable's Logic of The Specific and the Critique of the Global Village'. *Essay for the International Congress for the History of Religions.* Mexico City.

Heller, Agnes, 1996, *Seminario sobre la Modernidad.* Caracas: Doctorado de Ciencias Sociales, Universidad Central de Venezuela.

Jacinto Z., Agustin, 1995, 'Nishida Kitaro and Gutoko Shinram', *Essay for the International Congress for the History of Religion.* Mexico City.

Kuper, Adam, 1994, *The Chosen Primate.* Harvard Cambridge: Harvard – University Press.

Lopez-Sanz, Rafael, 1997, 'Cultura, Modernidad y Manifestaciones de Crisis', in *Venezuela: Tradicion y Modernidad.* Caracas: Fundacion Bigott – Universidad Simon Bolivar, pp. 99-107.

Manuel, Franz P. and Manuel, Fritzie, 1979, *Utopian Thought in the Western World.* Harvard-Massachusetts: Balknap Editors, Harvard University Press.

Man, Paul de, 1996, *The Resistance to Theory.* Manchester: University Press.

Marcus, George and M.J., Fisher, 1986, *Anthropology as Cultural Critique.* Chicago: The University of Chicago Press.

Munch, Richard, 1992, *Theory of Culture.* Berkeley: University of California Press.

Prigogine, Ilya, 1993, *Tan solo una ilusion?* Barcelona: Tusquet Editores (Orig. Fr. 1983).

Sahlins, Marshal, 1993, 'Good-bye to Tristes Tropos: Ethnography in the context of Modern World History', in *The Journal of Modern History,* Vol. 65, No. 1. March 1-26.

Stocking, George W., 1992, *The Ethnographers Magic and Other Essays in the History of Anthropology.* Wisconsin: University of Wisconsin Press.

TOWARD THE DEVELOPMENT OF ANTHROPOLOGY RELEVANT TO THE STUDY OF KOREAN PEOPLE, SOCIETY AND CULTURE

Han Sang-Bok

> *We may have to reorder our conception of urgent anthropology. Surely it should be the needs of mankind for the study of man that lead the way.*
>
> Laura Nader (1972: 308)

The purpose of this paper is to contribute to the development of anthropology relevant to the study of Korean people, society and culture. In this paper the 'relevance' of anthropology implies that anthropologists should situate themselves in relation to the issues they write about and that the discipline should not stray too far from the world in which real people live and work (Ahmed and Shore, 1995: 33). Before dealing with the main theme of the guidelines for the future development of Korean anthropology, I will examine the relevance of British, American and Chinese anthropologies to the social, economic and political situations in each of the countries in particular periods of time and I will also review the concept of Fei Xiaotong's 'people's anthropology' in connection with his anthropological research experiences and reflections during the period of more than 30 years when he was out of contact with his colleague anthropologists abroad.

In writing about the future for social anthropology, Raymond Firth (1992) raised a question concerning the relevance of theories and methods of the discipline developed in the West to the study of non-Western societies and cultures. The question has been asked: Given that increasing numbers of social anthropologists are likely to come from non-Western societies, will they approach the subject with assumptions and values different from those hitherto conventionally held? If so, will these be likely to change the fundamental nature of the discipline? He did not foresee such a fundamental change. I do not either, but I expect anthropology will develop towards the direction more relevant to the social realities in each country where historical background, socio-cultural situations and practically confronted problems are different. In fact, when we review the history of anthropology in the past, we can find that subjects, theories and methods of the discipline in each country have been varied in accordance with the realities and situations of the country. In looking forward to the nature of social science research in the future, while Anderson (1998: 31-33) stressed the significance of globalization and internationalization of social science and its practitioners in their devotions to public policy questions and contributions to solving the problems, in responding to this assertion, Kurien (1988: 36-37) indicated that the vast majority of social scientists will remain bounded to their particular disciplines and to their countries and localities.

- British, American And Chinese Cases

It is well known that British social anthropology was founded on the requirements of colonialism. As Kuklick (1991) described in the history of British anthropology, 1885-1945, all of the varieties of anthropologists including evolutionists, diffusionists and functionalists sought support for their work on the grounds that it would be useful for colonial administrators. As dominance of the discipline shifted from one school to another, colonial administrators confronted new problems and each school couched its appeals to its putative patrons in terms of their current needs. Because anthropologists' patrons agreed that Africa's colonial rulers needed expert guidance and were prepared to finance field research in Africa, the functionalist generation trained in the inter-war years was composed largely of Africanists.

The new research trends of culture and personality, acculturation and cultural ecology developed in American anthropology during the period from the 1920s to the 1930s also reflect the American social, economic and political situations in those times (Hatch, 1983). The general pessimism of the 1920s, the worldwide economic collapse of the 1930s and World War II stimulated a sense of crisis within the discipline. Thus culture and personality research focused on the relationship between culture and the human personality system and included such problems as the role of cultural institutions in the reduction of tension. Acculturation research sought to understand the impact of Western society on non-Western peoples and concentrated on such matters as the frustration and patterns of resistance and accommodation exhibited by the societies that were dominated. Cultural ecology set out to discover general patterns of cultural adaptation to environmental conditions.

The growth of the anthropological sciences in China is an exemplary one which shows us radical changes in the model of the discipline as social systems, ideologies and political forces change in the country. The Euro-American anthropology was adopted in China at the turn of this century. Since then by the 1940s, British social anthropology and American cultural anthropology had influenced the development of the discipline in China (Guldin, 1990, 1994). The anthropological sciences before 1949 were clearly set in a Western mould, or rather a number of Western moulds, but with the triumph of revolutionary forces the advisability of the entire Western perspective was placed in doubt and the Soviet model replaced it completely. With the Sino-Soviet split of the late 1950s and the radicalization of Chinese life, Mao Zedong's thought became the new standard by which to judge the social sciences' worth and this new yardstick was applied to anthropological work. The reforms of the 1980s turned anthropology into yet another track, this time emphasizing a Chinese model that incorporates foreign elements.

- Fei Xiaotong's 'People's Anthropology'

At the 40th annual meeting of the Society for Applied Anthropology, held in Denver, Colorado, U.S.A., Fei Xiaotong (1980, 1981: 1-19), as the recipient of Malinowski Memorial Award for 1980, delivered an address on people's anthropology. Recalling the advice of his mentor Malionwski, 'By all means go on with your study of Chinese society and its culture', Fei shared with his colleagues his anthropological research experiences and reflections during the period of more than 30 years after the Chinese people's revolution in 1949 in the following three aspects: One, how do we decide on the thing we are to investigate? Two, how do we investigators get along with the people we investigate? Three, what should be an investigator's attitude toward the effects of his investigation? According to his experiences, the three aspects of anthropological investigations before and after the people' revolution had become totally different as Chinese social and political situations changed.

First, before the people's revolution, the motive power of his investigations was the desire for national salvation from the ruthless grip of foreign imperialism and the feudal class at home and this became the theme of his investigation. After the victory of the people's revolution, however, the issue then confronting the Chinese people was how to rapidly turn China into a modern socialist country. Scientific knowledge was needed to tackle the problem and China's minority people became the subject and theme of his anthropological investigations. So his subjective wish was identified with the objective demand. The research work in which he participated answered the demands of the people living in the national minority areas and was geared to government's need to carry out its work for nationality affairs. In the course of his research work, the knowledge of comparative sociology and theories about the general law of social development were very useful in analyzing the minority societies. In other words, theory was linked with practice. The anthropologists tried to understand things and study theories for practical reasons. It was a good example of applied anthropology.

Second, when he undertook investigations in the countryside before liberation, he was frustrated because the people he investigated could not really understand why he made those investigations and what good they could do for them. Many people might have conceded that he meant no harm and so put up with his inquisitiveness but there were also people who grew suspicious and disliked his activities. Compared with his old research experience, after the liberation he found himself warmly received when he carried out his fieldwork among the minority people he investigated and they knew and believed that he meant to help, to help solve their problems so that what they dreamed of could come true.

Both parties of the investigators and the people under investigation were actually working hand in hand to observe and explain truthfully the existing social phenomena and problems, thereby enriching and deepening people's understanding of those phenomena and problems. In other words, the relations between investigators and the people changed radically. Anthropologists carried out their investigations entirely for the purpose of finding the way to bring about equality among nationalities and help the minority people forge ahead. It was also what the people were asking for. So anthropologists could be quite frank with the people about the purposes of investigations and the people perfectly understood what the investigations were for and found them acceptable. This new relationship between the investigator and the investigated provided the conditions enabling the former to gather materials that more truthfully reflected the actual state of affairs.

Third, anthropologists of the early generation generally did not concern themselves with the consequences of their investigations or their effects on the investigated and so the question of being responsible to the investigated did not arise. As to who was making use of their materials and for what purpose these materials were used and what would be the effects on the investigated, these questions seemed to be of no concern to anthropologists. But, after the liberation, it was necessary for anthropologists to estimate the effects of their work on society. This is not just a question of personal morality but also a question of what is good or bad for the majority of the people.

In short, what is meant by Fei Xiatong's people's anthropology is the investigation of people, society and culture which must be useful to the people and must be in keeping with serving the interests of the masses. And the ultimate goal of people's anthropology is to make the broad masses understand fully well the society they live in, to organize their collective life in accordance with existing social laws and to help satisfy their ever-growing needs.

• Guidelines For The Future Development Of Korean Anthropology

So far we examined the development of British, American and Chinese schools of anthropology relevant to the social, economic and political situations in each of the countries. Particularly Fei Xiaotong's new concept of people's anthropology may be characterized as a typical case of the relevance of anthropological investigation to the Chinese situations. Then, what are the guidelines for the future development of anthropology relevant to the study of Korean people, society and culture? To this question I would like to suggest the following five guidelines in connection with the relevance (Han, 1995): (1) the reform of anthropological infrastructure, (2) the enhancement of practical effectiveness of anthropology as a discipline, (3) the further development of anthropological theories and methods relevant to contemporary Korean situations, (4) the active participation of anthropologists in solving social problems and (5) the ethical issues encountered in anthropological fieldwork.

1. *Reform of anthropological infrastructure:* The institutional arrangements, education, training and organization of anthropologists are the major components of infrastructure related to the development of Korean anthropology. In Korea, there exist very limited number of research institutes, education and training facilities and posts for employment of anthropologists at work. Exchange programmes for education, training, research and academic organizations for professional anthropologists in Asia are underdeveloped. Despite the fact that social anthropology is an international discipline, regional associations like the European Association of Social Anthropologists and the Association of Social Anthropologists of Oceania have not been founded yet in Asia. Although the first international conference on

'Asian Peoples and Their Cultures' (Han, 1986) was held in Seoul, in 1980, to promote mutual cooperation and to share common problems and anthropological knowledge among Asian anthropologists, the next meeting has not been organized yet. These networks and other anthropological infrastructure should be reformed in order to facilitate the future development of both Korean and Asian anthropologies.

2. *Enhancement of practical effectiveness of anthropology as a discipline:* The proper career structure for professional anthropologists outside the academic field is lacking today in Korea. But in the future it is expected to increase the number of private, government and international agencies available for anthropologists. In order to provide for the future demand, more adequate education and training programmes are needed in applied as well as in academic fields of anthropology. It is necessary, for instance, to set up a short period course and to prepare appropriate curricula for basic training of vocational practice in anthropology. In fact, more support is being given for projects of an applied and policy-oriented rather than abstract theoretical order. Various funding agencies reinforce the interests of anthropologists in relating anthropology to practical problems such as environment, health and development in their research. The knowledge, as anthropologists' research results found from the local inhabitants through their hard work, should go back to the local inhabitants or serve to bring them a better life.
3. *Further development of anthropological theories and methods relevant to contemporary situations:* We have many anthropological theories and methods based on a variety of assumptions in the development of anthropology. These are not successive replacements of the old by the new ones, but corrective alternatives or complements. Since each of them is useful only in a particular context, none has ever seemed to me to be a completely satisfying theoretical statement. Thus, the existing anthropological theories and methods should be selected as an alternative, complemented, or modified into new one to be useful in the particular context of the study of Korean people, society and culture. It is expected that the Korean experts should exert all their possible efforts to develop a solid explanatory frame relevant to the study of Korean people and culture.
4. *Active participation of anthropologists in solving social problems:* It is

very important for anthropologists to convince the general public and policy makers that we have something substantial to offer in the solution of practical problems of Korean people, society and culture. It may be possible by means of research reports, writings, open lectures, or film presentations to a wider public and policy makers. To make the results of anthropological research more intelligible to the public and policy makers is clearly a short-cut to active participation in solving social problems. On the basis of careful analysis and explanation of complex social phenomena found in various action research projects, we may give warning of possible deleterious effects of proposed measures for social improvement, or we may ask the relevant questions to show where solutions may be found, if we cannot provide satisfactory solutions to social problems. In this way anthropologists can really contribute to an understanding of the human conditions in general and to solving practical social problems in particular. Now anthropology is being called upon more overtly to accept a notion of social responsibility. If anthropologists are to be supported from public funds, they must expect to be asked for some recognizable contribution to public benefit for the people rather than for the interests of the powerful. and they need to focus their work more on 'studying up' as Nader (1972) pointed out.

5. *Ethical issues encountered in anthropological fieldwork:* The more practical or pragmatic the issues that the anthropologist studies, the greater the pressures to conform to conventional norms of the community, firms, or organizations being studied by him are likely to be. To maintain our standards of honest reporting will demand ingenuity, persistence and even courage. In our presentations we anthropologists often find ourselves out of line with either our colleagues in other disciplines working in the same field, or with government officials or laymen trying to promote a particular policy. The anthropologist's presentation of a case study may be unexpected by authority and may be unpopular. In a particular project, the most unpopular finding of an anthropologist may be that there is no solution within the existing economic and political parameters laid down by the authorities. All that we can do in this case is to protest and try to expose the situation as widely as possible. Anthropologists must have social awareness, social conscience, some degree of commitment to the people among whom they work. An anthropologist

can sometimes defend the peoples' interests against bureaucratic ignorance, the rapacity of salesmen or the arrogance of developers.

Anyhow we must recognize our limitations both in research and practice. We must not become too disillusioned if we cannot change a social situation. Moreover, no degree of commitment should be allowed to blur one's judgement completely. The anthropologist's observational and analytical job is to preserve some freedom of evaluation and some relative abstraction from the situation. While there can be no absolute detachment (Firth, 1981) and no complete objectivity, a relative neutrality is quite possible in social anthropology. What is important to realize is that such relative detachment is not given automatically by anthropology itself. It has to be consciously sought and worked for, as an intellectual effort. The theme of relative objectivity is very important both in theory and practice.

REFERENCES

Ahmed, Akbar and Cris Shore(eds.), 1995, *The Future of Anthropology: Its Relevance to the Contemporary World.* London: Athlone.

Anderson, Lisa, 1988, 'Human Capital in the Social Sciences', in *Items* (Social Science Research Council) 52(2-3).

Fei, Xiaotong, 1980, 'Toward a People's Anthropology', in *Human Organization* 39(2). Washington D.C.: Society for Applied Anthropology.

Fei, Xiaotong, 1981, 'Toward a People's Anthropology', Beijing: New World Press.

Firth, Raymond, 1981, 'Engagement and Detachment: Reflections on Applying Social Anthropology to Social Affairs', in *Human Organization* 40(3). Washington D.C.: Society for Applied Anthropology.

——, 1992, 'A Future for Social Anthropology?', in *Contemporary Future: Perspective from Social Anthropology*, Sandra Wallman (ed.). London: Routledge.

Guldin, Gregory Eliyu, 1990, *Anthropology in China: Defining the Discipline.* Armonk. New York: M.E. Sharpe, Inc.

——, 1994, *The Sage of Anthropology in China: From Malinowski to Moscow to Mao,* Armonk, New York: M.E. Sharpe, Inc.

Han, Sang-Bok, 1986, *Asian Peoples and Their Cultures: Continuity and Change* (ed.). Seoul: Seoul National University Press.

——, 1995, 'The Relevance of Anthropological Theories to the Korean Society', in *Korean Cultural Anthropology* 28, Seoul: The Korean Society for Cultural Anthropology.

Hatch, Elvin, 1983, *Culture and Morality: The Relativity of Values in Anthropology.* New York: Columbia University Press.

Kuklick, Henrika, 1991, *The Savage Within: The Social History of British Anthropology, 1885-1945.* Cambridge: Cambridge University Press.

Kurien, C.T., 1998. 'Social Science and Social Reality', in *Items* (Social Science Research Council) 52(2-3).

Nader, Laura, 1972. 'Up the Anthropologist: Perspectives Gained from Studying Up', in *Reinventing Anthropology*, Dell Hymes (ed.). New York: Random House.

14

ALTERNATIVE PARADIGMS IN ANTHROPOLOGY AT THE CONFLUENCE OF CATEGORIES FROM INDIGENOUS AND GLOBAL KNOWLEDGE SYSTEMS

Jan Brouwer

• INTRODUCTION

For Anthropology the end of the 20th century is marked by a series of unfinished debates (emic/etic; culture/personality; modernity/post-modernity; and others). The discipline has been thoroughly in-disciplined to the extent of losing sight of the whole. It is hardly soothing to note that most social sciences and humanities find themselves in a similar situation. The problem is thus a general one. This justifies to place the problem in the wider perspective of the evolution of academic endeavours before proposing a way out. Here I make three observations : (i) the arts and sciences share the problem of observation, perception and objectivity; (ii) the arts precede sciences in opening new vistas; and (iii) the present crisis of interpretation is one of the hiccups of the post-atom era.[1]

Against this backdrop the social sciences in general and anthropology in particular have first to settle a few epistemological and methodological problems such as those related to the difference between knowledge and understanding, the axioms of science and the concept of holism. Ignorance of hidden biases and the cultural dimension of development have impeded anthropology at both the theoretical and applied levels.

Towards formulating an alternative paradigm in anthropology, I propose to make axioms and the concept of holism explicit in conjunction with an approach to data (whether European or non-European) from the broader perspective of the Indigenous Knowledge System to which they belong.

I illustrate the advantages of this new approach with examples from a case study on South Indian artisans. It shows at once, for academic purposes, an increased understanding of the phenomenon and for applied purposes the real baseline on which development programmes can be built.

• BACKGROUND TO THE CRISIS OF INTERPRETATION

The decade 1904-14 has in my view to be seen as a watershed in the European culture. Before this decade (and from A.D. 1435) the plastic arts were representational, the music was tonal, science had made advancements so that the 'twain - East and West - never met'. From this decade onwards the arts became visible, the music became a-tonal and in science the atom as a mini-constellation was discovered and thus 'the twain could meet'. Interestingly the arts have in all cases preceded science as if the arts had premonitions of what science was going to achieve.[2]

The reference to the arts is not without reason. What kept the arts busy, is what keep the sciences busy : The problems of observation, perception and objectivity. Between 1435 and 1472 Italian painters broke conventions prior to the Renaissance scientists.[3] The scientists of the Enlightenment period followed with major discoveries.[4]

During the European Middle Ages the supremacy of the Roman-Catholic church dictated an accent on the hereafter. The destination of the human soul was to be found in the hereafter. The following movement of Humanism moved the centre of gravity to life on earth now (*hic et nunc*). The present in terms of Space and Time is the reality which the individual (the 'I') perceives through his senses.

Seven years after the painter Masaccio, the painter Alberti perfected perspective painting based on one own's visual observations in AD 1435. His motto was : 'The way I see things, is the way things are. If you stand in my place you will see it the same way'. In other words the fixed point of our eye became the reference for the horizon. However, anybody knew, that the line from eye to horizon is fictitious and moves with the standpoint of the individual vertically.

Alberti's breakthrough in the perception of Space and Time was thus not objective. It announced, so to speak, the scientific discoveries of the Enlightenment.

Similarly Dali's first Surrealism (1904), Picasso's first abstract painting (1907) and Schoenberg's 12-tone system (1911) announced the 'discovery' of the concept of the atom by Niels Bohr (1913).

Thus, the arts expressed new ways of looking at the world. We do not know much about the trigger mechanisms at work. But it seems that a process of collective rethinking is going on and first expresses in the arts and then more concretely in science.

Since the Renaissance the chief principles were : 'Sensory experience is the mother of all security' and 'All true science is the result of experience through the five senses' (Leonardo da Vinci, AD 1500).

During the past four centuries the natural sciences were guided by 'The conviction that all existence in the Universe in general and the existence of each thing in particular makes up the absolute reality' (Huizinga).

However, in the 20th century the same natural sciences discovered that for a precise definition of reality the senses are not enough.

Ever since the scientific discoveries of the early 20th century, the observations on which the natural science work was founded since the Renaissance proved not to be objective at all. In the 20th century the logic is extended : 'The things outside ourselves become inside ourselves a perception of reality through a process of interference by the vibrations of the outside world and those of our inner world' (Bergson, 1900).

The series of scientific discoveries, notably that the smallest particle, the atom, is not material, but a planetary system of electrical loads, strips the plastic arts of their perspectives, the music of its scales, the dance of its classical ballet and drama of its grandiloquencies.

As early as AD 1913 the German philosopher Husserl stated that '(a) one observes always only parts and never simultaneous the totality; and (b) things show themselves to man in many aspects; it depends on the circumstances how certain parts manifest themselves'. In other words, 20th century science recognises the *coincidentia oppositorium.*

The implications of the breakthrough, visible in arts and tangible in science, are also reflected in the other domains of society, notably the political domain.

The foregoing outline on the European history of observation and objectivity may serve as a background to the development in the political domain and in the social sciences during the 20th century.

Whatever the political and economical compulsions might have been, European thinking was shattered after the 1904-14 decade. The end of the colonial period was both empirically and cognitively immanent.

'It was, however, not until the incisive book by Edvard Said, *Orientalism* (1978), that the study of literature, the arts and the social sciences was seen to be inscribed in the framework of the European colonial adventure and enterprise' (Assayag, 1997). Although Said's work suffers form factual errors and the technique of anachronism, it engendered the project of rethinking, the problem of the construction of the other as much in disciplines of fiction as in the field of social sciences.

• The Post-Atom Era and Anthropology

Thus, the discovery of the atom and even later discoveries that the atom is not the smallest unit, have literally and metaphorically broken down all that was thought of as achieved. Baudrillard had rightfully argued that the problem for the USA is 'the crises of an achieved utopia, confronted with the problems of its duration and permanence' (Baudrillard, 1988 : 77). For Europe, the post-atom era is one of the perceptions of never having achieved anything.[5] It is then not surprising that such academic disciplines as Indology, History, Anthropology, Sociology, Developmental Studies, etc. find themselves in a crisis of interpretation. The post-orientalism and post-modernity debate may serve as a witness, particularly through the works of Dirks, Inden, Marriot and Said. However, the post-modernity debate appears to me as a cyclically recurring attempt towards an axial breakthrough of European axiomas underlying most of the social science research. The proposed approaches to non-European material need to be studied only in its own terms. The result of unrelated cultural entities reminds us of the European perception of its own society.

Most social science programmes have to do with the extent to which Indian society approximates the characteristics of market economies, or more generally, with studies of Indian society in terms of economic categories. For nearly fifty years, research and development projects are being conducted in the Indian subcontinent virtually ignoring two major signals warning the development initiatives against lack of impact as a result of underestimation of a cultural approach or an overestimation of self-proclaimed objectivity.

The first signal was given by Sahlins who summarized the two basic assumptions that underlie programmes or projects as : (i) 'The cultural order is to be conceived as a codification of man's actual purposeful and pragmatic action; (ii) human action in the world is to be understood as mediated by the cultural design, which gives order at once to practical experience, customary practice and the relationship between the two' (Sahlins 1976 : p.55).

The second signal came from the international symposium on the cultural dimension of development held in The Hague in 1985 under the auspices of the UNESCO. In his keynote address, Professor Kottak of Ann Anbor, observed that 'One of the most significant findings of my comparative study of development projects was that the average economic rates of return for culturally compatible projects were much higher than those for incompatible ones. In other words, attention to the cultural dimension pays off in financial terms, in rates of return twice as high as those for culturally insensitive projects' (Kottak, in Uhlenbeck, 1985 : p.38).

From both the academic and humanitarian points of view, it is said that only a few individual scholars and development workers and institutions have had the courage to change the crop patterns in the plains of the social sciences.

It is remarkable that historians, more than sociologists or anthropologists, are sensitive to the multidimensional and multidisciplinary approach, which paves the way at once for the required understanding of society and justice for the human agency. 'It is likely that even the most esoteric social anthropological report will produce at least some information of interest to development economists' (Epstein, 1978, p.6).

Ignoring the social constitution, the cultural formation and the meaning of economy results in an approach to the data from the vantage point of declared universal truths. Reasons for these approaches have to be sought in the peculiar European divisions which culminated in the superiority of the economic domain in European societies. Whatever may be the relationship between the economic and other domains of European society, a serious study of economic cases outside Europe has to take the indigenous construction of cases into account.

Given the non-sustainability of many of the development projects, which often means intervention of modern technological practices, the Indigenous Knowledge approach to development can show a way out of the impasse. Raj's argument against the expectation that technology alone can provide increased productivity and that particular institutional changes are needed, is curiously correct (Raj, 1990 : 20-21, 44-45).

The study of Indigenous knowledge systems brings the localistic data from artisans, farmers and others back to the semantics of the participants' own discourse away from folklore.

To overcome this problem, the cognized social knowledge is to be understood with the help of cumulative knowledge and an awareness of heterotopia. Cumulative knowledge is not simply additive, but is knowledge accumulated horizontally, covering various conventionally segregated disciplines and a vertically relevant historical past. The understanding is reached by a juxtaposition and comparison conceived by heterotopia. This holistic approach leads to the construction of a space in which policy recommendations can be created that transcend the moment of their making.

Social science and the epistemological assumptions upon which it is based can be redefined in the aforementioned way. Thus it is able to identify a structural condition for unprecedented knowledge and understanding on which policy recommendations can also be based.

The modern state's definition of 'development' is a monolithic, unidirectional and singularly economic concept. By contrast, the indigenous concept of 'development' is a multi-directional, pluralistic concept covering different domains simultaneously - the economic, the ritual, the political — and is worded in a religious term, namely, 'purity'.

The two concepts are thus not only contrasted, but the indigenous concept encompasses the modern concept at the same time. The more comprehensive nature of the indigenous concept stands therefore open to certain aspects of the modern concept. The openness or flexibility of indigenous society gives opportunities for modern development to find its niche in or among the indigenous developments. It is therefore justified to speak of 'alternative in developments' rather than 'alternatives in development'. The latter formulation expresses the need for different models as the modern concept of development ignores the indigenous concept of development and its alternatives.

• Indigenous Knowledge And Understanding

The concept of Indigenous Knowledge in the social sciences was not somehow lost in the debate which centered around the epistemological dilemma between the native voice and the anthropological vision.[6]

The term native simply refers 'to people who at some point are studied by social anthropologists as inhabitants of a particular social space' (Hastrup, 1993 : 174). All of us are natives in some mould of a defined temporal and social space. In this context, Vendler (1984) and Hastrup (1993) recognize the difference between knowing and understanding or between 'an intimate and implicit native knowledge and external and explicit expert understanding' (Hastrup, 1993:175).

The participants' knowledge of their temporal and social space is what the anthropologist understands as the *Indigenous Knowledge*. The latter's detached analytical understanding may recognize their Indigenous Knowledge Systems. The study of Indigenous Knowledge System is an attempt to bridge knowing and understanding. For, a genuine anthropological understanding remains different from mere knowing.

In this context, the anthropological method of holism is a particular kind of epistemology. Holism then is to acknowledge 'the human agency or the capacity of people to order their world' (Inden, 1990 : 1).

There is a fundamental difference between the 'human agency' and the anthropologist. The human agency has an intimate and sometimes implicit knowledge, but it does not have the knowledge of how culture is constituted. Tyler gives an apt analogy by stating that 'Knowing a language does not mean knowing rules and structures, but knowing how to make oneself understood' (Tyler, 1978:120).

Although this dichotomy remains, the study in which the Indigenous Knowledge Systems are premised and exploited as resources, will provide a new kind of knowledge in the social sciences. In postmodern studies, holism no longer claims the totality from the outside, but 'it is experienced from inside with the aim of learning how people construct, change and deconstruct their own social spaces' (Hastrup, 1993:181).

The holistic study of Indigenous Knowledge Systems, then, creates an unprecedented prophetic condition in the sense of incipient change.

- Axiom Of Science And Holism

In the forgoing section, I have argued in favour of recognition of the human agent, diversity of culture and the reinvention of holism to advance social science knowledge. However, in our field of studies, scholars rarely make their axioms explicit.

Modern science is axiomatic in its conception of Nature as distinct from Culture. Hence, Culture can study Nature. Among anthropologists, Bernard Cohn was perhaps the first to recognise this. In 1978 he wrote : 'All culture is constructed. It is the product of human thought. Since culture is always being constituted and constructed, so it is also always being transformed.... It is only through culture that we construct nature, not the other way round' (Cohn, 1992, p. 43 [1987] originally written in 1978). The separation between Nature and Culture occurred in the 17th and 18th centuries. At that time, scientific knowledge began to win the battle against contemporary mythical and mystical thought. Science, it was believed, could only exist after an axial breakthrough, the perception that knowledge is to be perceived through the senses. 'Thanks to this separation scientific thought was able to constitute itself' (Levi-Strauss, 1989:6). Now, at the turn of the 20th century, science, or more precisely social science, is more and more attempting to integrate local knowledge in the field of scientific explanation. Western perspective regards Nature as 'a linear phenomenon in which what happens in a given place and time is determined exclusively by what has occurred at nearby places immediately beforehand' (Barrow, 1991:13). In other words, Western social science is also axiomatic in its belief in cause-effect thinking within a single logical domain of reference.

These axioms made it possible to divide Nature and Culture into different fields of study to the extent of losing sight of the whole. The holistic approach then is to consider the structural relationships of various such fields from the vantage point of a scope of investigation.

It has to be borne in mind that this is significantly different from much of the non-Western sciences, in which the holistic view assumes Nature to be intrinsically non-linear, so that 'non-local influences predominate and interact with one another to form a complicated whole' (Barrow, 1991:13).

No scientific research is free from axioms and making them explicit in the social sciences, will be helpful in the recognition of the difficulties of recording and analyzing indigenous knowledge in its holistic form.

• From A Case Study On South Indian Artisans[7]

The case study was concerned with the artisans of the Visvakarma caste of Karnataka in South India. This caste comprises of blacksmiths, carpenters, coppersmiths, sculptors and goldsmiths. Their oral tradition (speech, narratives, secret crafts lexicon) and actions in their crafts formed the resources on which analysis and reconstruction are based.

The problems that the Visvakarma artisans face in the world with the unavoidable cooperation of external agents and the delivery of the product are a direct result of their ideal of being placed outside the world. The key concept of their ideology is completeness (*paripurnata*).

The crux of the concept of 'completeness' stems from the fact that the ideal is located outside the world as in the values of renunciation which deny the reality of the social order for which the Visvakarmas manufacture their products. Therefore, the Visvakarmas conceptualize the Self (as a group) and Society in terms of a transcendent completeness. On the boundaries of the transcendent order of the Self and the mundane order of Society, the Goddess Kali is drawn to square the circle of completeness by her dynamic effectiveness.

The answer to the question as to why Kali is the chosen deity, is to be sought in the Visvakarma view on Self and Society. This view is visible in the so-called handbills, which are printed handouts explaining the structure of the caste by means of about 45 variables including the Five Elements (*panchabhuta*). It is also visible in their secret crafts lexicon, or *adurubasha*, which I have discussed elsewhere (Brouwer, 1997b and forthcoming). The handbills are exegeses of the Visvakarma caste tradition in the image of the single body with the five heads, associating the total

Visvakarma with the Five Elements of Life. In the handbills, as well as in the origin stories of the caste, the total Visvakarma is depicted in terms of knowledge also coded as Space (*akasa*), in contrast to all ignorant others (Brouwer, 1995a, 1995b). The lexicon classifies the Self in spatial terms in contrast to the others of Society who are classified in temporal terms, notably those directly, or indirectly, referring to Death.[8]

Thus, the Goddess mediates between the Visvakarma and Society, or between Life and Death. The Goddess Kali, whose dual nature may be summarized as Death-causing and Life-giving, is the logical choice from the pantheon.

The typical Visvakarma perception of Self and Society leads, on the micro level of the economic domain, to a different kind of dynamics in society. Here the spatial division is between the secular (for transcendent act of the craft) and the sacred (for Society of humans and deities). In the temporal division of the crafts, the assignments are divided and spread over time; on the occupational level, the division of labour points to a single network of producers and consumers.

Schematically the actions of the five craftsmen can be presented thus : the product of the blacksmith is the Goddess and she moves from the Self/ Life to Society/Death. It is her movement and not society that gives the blacksmith his money. The blacksmith's product is perfect and thus no ceremonies are required.

At the other end of the scale, there is the goldsmith who delivers the product to the Goddess who then delivers it herself to the customer. It is through her that the goldsmith receives money.

This observation calls for a closer look at the Kannada Visvakarma goldsmith's connections with his customer. From him he receives gold in the form of old jewellery to make new jewellery. At the time of delivery, the finished product is placed on a corner of the forge from where the customer takes it. Here, the crux of the matter is that the forge (*aggistike*) is an image of the Goddess. It is thus the Goddess who mediates between the goldsmith and society. The triangular connection is marked by the following movements : (i) money and used gold, move from the customer to the goldsmith; (ii) the finished product moves from the goldsmith to the Goddess and then from the Goddess to the customer. The goldsmith is thus under great obligation to her.

More often than not it happens that the goldsmith delays the delivery of the product. There are various worldly, if not trivial reasons for such delays.

The important point is, however, the goldsmith's view on delay. How does he cope with it? His answer is simple : he prays to the Goddess for help. In case of no delay he prays to thank her. The delay itself is, significantly, a matter of time.

The other important connection is the one the goldsmith has with the Shroff. The goldsmith receives principal raw material from the Shroff, as well as money. He thus receives the Goddess (in her material manifestation) and does not return the gesture. He cannot and should not present a gift to the Shroff, as the latter, like all non-Visvakarmas, belongs to Society (Death).

This observation has two implications : (i) the goldsmith returns the gift from the Goddess by offering presentations to her temple in the direction of ever flowering life, while (ii) the money received from 'Death' terminates the relationship of exchange.

From the Shroffs I learned that the goldsmiths never actually repay loans that they have given to them. (The average outstanding loan is about Rs. 30,000 per goldsmith per year.) Of course, the goldsmith cannot repay a loan, for this would imply a form of reciprocity which once received would end the social relation attached to it. Would he repay the loan, it would mean recognition of the relationship. On the other hand, the Shroff is not keen on repayment of outstanding loans. For him it is through lending debts that he has command over men and more precisely, over the best goldsmiths.

In this context, it is also possible to deduce the views on profit. The Shroff makes his profit (*labh*) by buying gold at cheaper rates than the official one and by selling jewellery to his customers. He thus makes profit at both ends of the process of a deal. The margin of his profit links him with society. In the Shroff's view, money creates a relationship : the more he pays the goldsmith, he thinks, the better and more he will work for him; the smaller the margin at selling time, the better his relationship with the customer.

In contrast to the time of profit making by the Shroff, the goldsmith makes his profit within the process of manufacturing (the wastage [*tyamana*] and the wages [*majuri*]). Together wastage and wages are his profit called *labhadevi*, which literally means 'added by the Goddess'. The temporal process of transformation of substance (gold) into form (product) is thus the result of a cosmic exchange between the male and female constituent parts of the universe and not the result of a worldly transaction.

The foregoing analysis of the Visvakarmas in the world demonstrates that the metaphysical, religious, economic, social and political domains are intertwined. No domain functions on its own. A specific economic aspect of the indigenous concept of completeness relates to the evolving chain of 'finished' though incomplete jobs. This chain guarantees income generation. In the case of the goldsmith, the delay is a risk, as the price of gold may go up or down. The concept may thus be also part of a larger corpus of concepts making for an indigenous survival strategy.

The perception of society in terms of intertwined domains follows directly from the world-view. As the case of the Visvakarmas demonstrates, the transcendent order is the order of virtues, completeness and perfection, for which qualities there is no place in the world.

The Visvakarma views his authority as being of a transcendent nature, which vindicates his power position in society (as makers of the world). Although in his view his power is thereby accepted, it is to be made effective by the legitimation of the Goddess.

Modern development discourse, whether from the vantage point of sociology, economy, or political sciences, is axiomatic in the universal validity of such categories as 'money', 'profit' and 'debt'. By isolating and prioritizing the economic domain, which is characteristic of the European perception of society, they conclude, in so-called objective terms and categories, that local economies are underdeveloped and need intervention to bring them into main- stream economy. Whether such studies are Weberian or Marxist, they have in common the *a priori* boundaries and terms of comparison.

The human agents of change, such as those designing development projects for artisans, as well as conventional anthropologists, sociologists and historians have commonly fallen into the trap of attributing to money a set of meanings emanating from their own culture. Ignoring the relevant concepts behind local practices in Indigenous Knowledge Systems is then an impediment for development.

My endeavour to analyse regularities and reconstruct indigenous categories out of seemingly unique and haphazard local interactions leads in particular to the artisans' concept of money. In contrast to the modern conception of money as a means to create a relationship, e.g. between employer and employee, the indigenous view of exchange considers money by contrast as a means to terminate relationships. For groups like the artisans studied here, the repayment of a debt would then mean the acceptance of a mutual obligation, or rather a dependence on society entailing a complete undermining of their social position and chosen way to prosperity and liberation.

The Visvakarma perception of society in terms of Death seems not to be an isolated one. For Galey demonstrated that the debts of men resemble debt towards death and that the world is ordered by debt. The relationship between death, debt and society seems to be a key perception in the Indian Indigenous Knowledge Systems.

The differential response of Indian artisans to modern macroeconomic possibilities and to specific development projects for the artisanal sector could not be understood for academic as well as applied purposes on the basis of socio-economic studies alone. Therefore, the sociological study was complemented by an anthropological study focusing on the rationale of artisans' choices (see Brouwer, 1996). This led to a search for the meaning of economic concepts based on the axiom of the modern concept of artisan and the concept of holism from the global categories and the concept of the Five Elements (*panchabhuta*) from the Indian categories (see Brouwer, 1997b). At the confluence of categories of the global and local knowledge systems, the studies revealed relevant perceptions of society and indigenous economic concepts which are significantly different from those on which conventional social sciences are based (see Brouwer, 1997a and forthcoming).

• Towards An Alternative Paradigm

Here, I argue that ignoring the indigenous knowledge system, in design and implementation of development projects, is an impediment for sustainability of development. This does not mean that there is no change. Rural transformation does take place, but it is neither a series of events nor a directory of requirements. First, two types of change are to be recognised : (i) the ongoing process of transformation in society as defined by its own domains and (ii) a transformation as a result of osmosis between the indigenous and modern perception of society.

Most transformation studies depend on hidden assumptions or *a priori* definitions rooted in the Western perceptions of society, State and change. Such overt or covert starting points carry, more often than not, the pretension of universal truths. Comparison, then, takes place at one step too early. An understanding of the indigenous general and specific, as well as the unique and universal of the Modern State, is required before cross-cultural comparison leads to valid conclusions.

To arrive at a general scientific knowledge 'out of place' and 'out of time', the point of departure is the reality of the particular. In other words, the social scientist relativises the participants' knowledge on his way to scientific objectification.

This does not necessarily imply that the indigenous and modern concepts are always at loggerheads. There are differential correspondences and discrepancies depending on the social, cultural and regional contexts. Individual approaches, such as the functional, structural, dialectical and interpretative should not be isolated, as function, structure, dialectics and interpretation are also constituent parts of Indian culture. This is not to say that Indian reality should be studied through a purely indigenous approach as this 'would end up in cultural solipsism and myopia' (Ostor, 1984:197). Rather the approach should be undertaken at the confluence of social science, history, Indology and other disciplines. Specific Indian concepts, such as 'completeness' and 'purity', which Indians employ in the semantic fields of social and economic problems can never be used in theories at global knowledge levels. They are, however, indispensable for their and our understanding of the Indian field of ethnological study.

Serious studies of Indigenous Knowledge Systems of which the Indigenous Technical Knowledge is an expression, are attempts to fight Eurocentrism about which Herzfeld wrote : 'As a European-originated discipline, anthropology cannot evade the Eurocentric character of its criterion of comparison. It oscillates between this cultural heritage on the one hand and an equally potent yearning to escape the constraints of bias altogether on the other' (Herzfeld, 1989:18).

For such studies, whether aimed at deepening anthropological understanding or founding a solid baseline for development policies, have to combine concepts taken from both the universal and culture – specific categories.

The collection and authentication of Indigenous Knowledge in its cognitive and practical dimensions at the confluence of concepts originating in different knowledge systems with active people's participation in collection and preservation, can give them back their history and full potential for coping with changing scenarios.

NOTES

1. This paper has grown out of discussions at three different seminars, namely : On IK and Sustainable Development at CARIKS (Mysore, 1994); Colloquium at CNRS (Paris, 1994); and Evolving Perspectives for Development Studies at Goa (1997). I am greatly indebted to Jean-Claude Galey, Sashi Hegde and James Heimann for having helped me shaping my ideas. Naturally I remain responsible for the text as it is now.

2. The concept of the atom (*a-tomos* in Greek) was first formulated by Heraklites (544–483 BC). Niels Bohr's atom model (AD 1913) was a hypothesis based on calculations, not observations.
3. Leon Battista Alberti, in his work 'On Painting', discusses perspective painting and anatomy in AD 1435.
4. The references to the arts would never have been made without the deep insights of my teacher for the History of Art, Dr. Mrs. O.L. Bouma in The Hague. I am greatly indebted to her.
5. The European self-perception of 'never have achieved anything' is, of course, an achievement in itself. This insight in its own insufficiency is not only modest, but opens the culture up for an exchange of thought with other cultures. This is increasingly visible in the new East-West relationships.
6. As regards India, anthropological critique has suggested that we are 'Imagining India' or should work towards an 'Indian Sociology'. For India, the debate opened with Inden's attack not only on Indian historiography and anthropology, but on the human sciences in general. His call for the exploration of activities where the agency cannot be ignored, should be taken to heart by any social scientist, whether engaged in pure or development oriented research. Where Inden's imagination is at places too powerful (we are waiting for more and more elaborate 'Reconstructions'), McKim Marriott appears to take a short cut by proposing the construction of an Indian ethno-sociology, or more precisely a sociology through Hindu categories. Apart from the difficulty that there are various Hindu ways of thinking, his enterprise seems to lead to the replacement of one bias by another.
7. For a complete analysis of the case, see Brouwer, 1997.
8. The secret crafts lexicon covers at least the following areas : (i) Categorical terms : such as place, time, good, bad, pure, impure, right, left, gift; (ii) craft-related terms : such as those for raw materials, tools, assets, processes of manufacture and delivery of products; (iii) terms referring to people : such as names of castes, sub-castes, tribes, ancestors; and (iv) terms relating to customs : such as those for non-vegetarian food, alcoholic drinks.

REFERENCES

Assayag, Jackie, *et al.*, 1997, *Orientalism and Anthropology : From Max Mueller to Louis Dumont*. Pondy Papers in Social Sciences, 24.

Baudrillard, Jean, 1988. *America*. London: Verso.

Barrow, John D., 1991, *Theories of Everything: The Quest For Ultimate Explanation.* London: Vintage.

Brouwer, Jan, 1996, 'Units of Production in South India : An Explanation of Artisans' Choices' in *Production Units in Micro and Macro Structural Perspectives,* Burton Stein (ed.). Delhi: Oxford University Press.

Brouwer, Jan, 1997a, 'The Goddess for Development. Indigenous Economic Concepts among South Indian Artisans', in *Social Anthropology*,5,I.

——, 1997b, 'The Artisans Oral Tradition as a Resource of History', in *Actes du Colloque*. Pondicherry: IFP/EFEO.

——, (forthcoming), *Indigenous Knowledge of South Indian Smiths and Weavers in Development Perspective*. (IDPAD, 1996).

Cohn, S. Bernard, 1992 (1987), *An Anthropologist among the Historians and Other Essays* (1978). Delhi: Oxford University Press.

Epstein, T. Scarlett, 1973, *South India – Yesterday, Today and Tomorrow*. London: Macmillan Press Ltd.

Hastrup, Kristen, 1993, 'The Native Voice and the Anthropological Vision', in *Social Anthropology*, 1,2, pp.173-85.

Herzfeld, Michael, 1988, *Anthropology Through the Looking-Glass : Critical Ethnography in the Margins of Europe*. Cambridge : Cambridge University Press.

Inden, Ronald, 1990, *Imagining India*. Oxford: Oxford University Press.

Kolff, Dirk H.A., 1990, *Naukar, Rajput and Sepoy : The Ethno-history of the Military Labour in Hindustan, 1450-1850*. Cambridge : Cambridge University Press.

Levi-Strauss, Claude, 1989, *Myth and Meaning*. The 1977 Massey Lectures. London : Routledge.

Marriott, McKim, 1990, 'Constructing an Indian Ethnosociology', in *India through Hindu Categories*. New Delhi: Sage Publications.

Ostor, Akos, 1984, *Culture and Power: Legend, Ritual, Bazaar and Rebellion in a Bengali Society*. New Delhi: Sage Publications.

Raj, K.N., 1990, *Organizational Issues in Indian Agriculture*. Delhi.

Sahlins, Marshall, 1976, *Culture and Practical Reason*. Chicago: University of Chicago Press.

Said, E., 1978, *Orientalism*. New York : Pantheon.

Tyler, Stephen, 1978, *The Said and the Unsaid : Mind, Meaning and Culture*. New York: Academic Press.

Uhlenbeck, G.C., ed., 1985, *The Cultural Dimension of Development*. The Hague: Netherlands National Commission for UNESCO.

Vendler, Zeno, 1984, 'Understanding People', in *Culture Theory, Essays on Mind, Self and Emotion*. R.A. Schweder and A. Levine, (eds.) Cambridge: Cambridge University Press.

INDEX

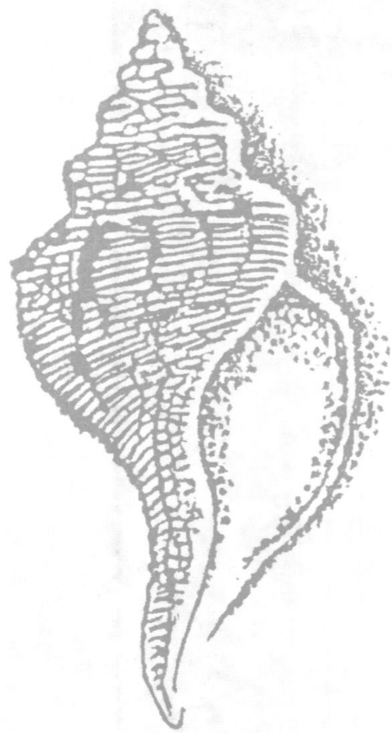